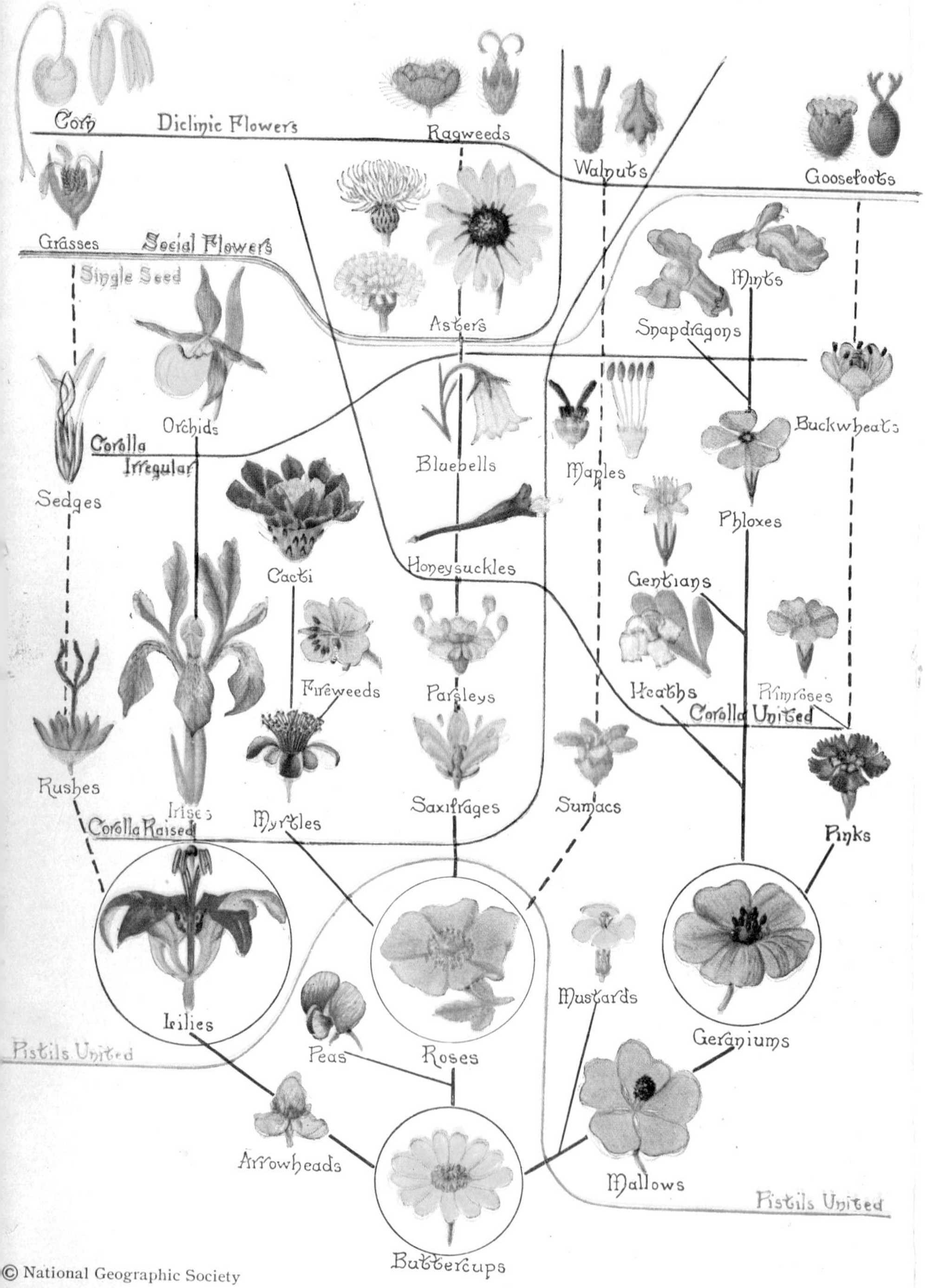
Corn
Diclinic Flowers
Ragweeds
Walnuts
Goosefoots
Grasses
Social Flowers
Single Seed
Asters
Mints
Snapdragons
Orchids
Corolla
Irregular
Bluebells
Maples
Buckwheats
Sedges
Phloxes
Cacti
Honeysuckles
Gentians
Fireweeds
Parsleys
Heaths
Primroses
Corolla United
Rushes
Irises
Myrtles
Saxifrages
Sumacs
Pinks
Corolla Raised
Lilies
Roses
Mustards
Geraniums
Peas
Pistils United
Arrowheads
Mallows
Pistils United
Buttercups

FLOWER CHART

FLOWERS OF COAST AND SIERRA

WITH THIRTY-TWO PLATES IN COLOR

By

EDITH S. CLEMENTS, PH.D.

CARNEGIE INSTITUTION OF WASHINGTON

THE H. W. WILSON COMPANY

NEW YORK

1928

Printed in the United States of America

W.B.CONKEY
COMPANY

CONTENTS AND ILLUSTRATIONS

PREFACE

The present book is designed for the nature lover who wishes to know something of the wild-flowers, but who is deterred by the difficulty of keys and the technicality of descriptions in the manuals, and by the inadequacy of illustration in popular books on the subject. For those who are interested only in the names of plants, it is hoped that the thirty-two plates will be sufficient to supply this information. They are as accurate representations as the limitations of the method permit, not only as to form and color but actual size as well, and all are drawn and painted from life. A special effort has been made to select the most attractive and fitting common name from those already in use, and also to indicate its appropriateness. Where there is no distinctive common name, it is suggested that the name of the genus be brought into popular usage, as has already been done for iris, geranium and chrysanthemum. The scientific name appears in a parenthesis for certainty of identification, and it is also analyzed as an aid to memory or as a matter of historical interest.

For those who desire more than a mere knowledge of plant names, the text is planned to give information as to relationship, distribution, uses and the inter-actions between flowers and insects. While the illustrations are limited to a little more than two hundred of the most beautiful or familiar flowers of the Pacific Coast, from southern California to British Columbia, mention is made of many others in the same region, as well as of related species found elsewhere in the country. Brief family paragraphs concern cognate genera in other parts of the world and likewise indicate the outstanding differences and similarities of neighboring families. An endeavor has been made to present the facts in a readable manner, and no apology is offered for the frequent use of metaphor.

Acknowledgments are due the National Geographic Society for generous permission to use the colored plates which were originally made for the National Geographic Magazine and appeared in the May number, 1927; to Dr. Harvey M. Hall of the Carnegie Institution of Washington for the identification of doubtful species and material for illustration, and to Dr. Frederic E. Clements of the Carnegie Institution of Washington for information, suggestions and criticisms throughout the preparation of the book.

EDITH S. CLEMENTS.

Mission Canyon,
Santa Barbara,
June 10, 1928.

INTRODUCTION

Many million years ago when this staid old earth was still in its turbulent youth; when vast mountain ranges were being lifted and oceans were shrunken into their basins; when giant tree-ferns and horse-tails had passed their prime and huge reptiles browsed on the shores of lakes and streams—then were evolved from their fern-like ancestors the first plants that bore true flowers. This simple first step gave no hint at the time of the vast host of beautifully colored blossoms and specialized forms that were to develop through the ages, step by step, under the influence of changing climates and environments.

The princely savage who is able to recite the names of two hundred ancestors, and his white brother who proudly traces his descent for many generations, are mere parvenus in comparison with the most advanced flowering plants. In terms of experience as well as of time, it is a long ways from "King Corn," representing the extreme of specialization, back to the earliest buttercups that were pioneers in solving the problems of the continued existence of themselves and their offspring. They had few precedents to go by, little knowledge handed down from the past. Their success or failure depended entirely upon the outcome of experiments and of consequent reactions to changing conditions and recurring emergencies in daily living.

Some of the buttercups were conservatives that remained in the same environment from generation to generation and retained their ancestral form and structure. Others varied with the changing climate, as new factors acted upon them. It may have been that an increase in the rainfall caused the disappearance of those too fixed to respond to the change, while the more adaptable became plants of swamp and stream. On the other hand, some seasons may have been so unfavorable to bees and butterflies that their absence resulted in the elimination of such flowers as failed to adjust themselves to the lack of insect pollinators. Those blossoms that happened to possess lighter pollen were better fitted to survive by reason of its being carried by the wind, and also, little by little, to increase it in amount and lightness so that it became more and more easily carried. The pollen must have increased at the expense of the corolla, since practically all wind-pollinated flowers lack this part which had become useless in the change from insect attraction.

It is also quite possible that at some time in the history of flowers, there were an unusual number of bees and butterflies in the environment. As a consequence the weight of the insect visitor, as it alighted more often on a petal or pushed harder and harder at the nectar glands, resulted in changing the shape of the flower, and irregular forms such as those of the columbine and monkshood were developed from regular buttercups.

Thus, through the ages, some factor in the environment—rain, drouth, wind, insects, heat, cold—has had its effect. Those flowers that failed to adapt themselves disappeared from the face of the earth, while such as met the conditions successfully became gradually differentiated, until today the plant kingdom comprises an innumerable host of different kinds of flowers. Their relationship to each other and course of development can be traced in the light of changes still taking place in accordance with known laws and processes. These are employed by the horticulturalist and plant breeder in the production of still newer forms and varieties. They are the same processes that have produced the Japanese chrysanthemum from the wild species and the durum wheats from a wild grass, and although the results are more rapid and certain under controlled conditions, the influences are the same that have worked upon plant protoplasm since its beginning.

Probably the earliest attempt to arrange flowering plants into related groups was made by Aristotle, when he distinguished them as trees, shrubs and herbs. He was followed by classifiers who based their systems on the characters of roots, stems and leaves, and it was not until the seventeenth century that the importance of the flower as the basis of a natural classification was perceived. This idea has been developed by many successive workers in the field of systematic botany, until it is here presented in the graphic form of the flower chart, or family tree of the flowers. This aims to express as clearly and simply as possible the general lines of evolution, and hence of relationship, of the most important groups of flowering plants known today. It has the additional advantage in this form of providing a short-cut to the recognition of flower families, and eliminates the need for the longer and more difficult technical family keys in the manuals.

The flower chart is based upon the principles of a starting point, the buttercups; three great centers, geraniums, roses and lilies, and two lines of development from each of the centers. These related but diverging lines of evolution are a result of the two forces at work upon the flower: insects and wind, culminating in the former case in the orchids, sunflowers and mints, and in the latter in the goosefoots, walnuts and grasses. In the insect-pollinated flowers the corolla has been the part primarily affected, while in the wind-pollinated ones the emphasis has been put upon the stamens and pistils, with the resulting loss of corolla and often of calyx also. The broken black lines represent the course of development of the wind-pollinated flowers from each of the three centers, and the unbroken lines indicate that of the insect-pollinated flowers from the same points.

The important changes that have taken place in the process of evolution are indicated on the chart by colored cross-lines. The first four of these concern the insect-pollinated flowers, three of them affecting the corolla, while the last three include wind-pollinated flowers also. These steps of advance took place at different times in the three lines and hence cross them at different points.

The arrangement of the flowers of the Pacific Coast, in the discussion following, is based upon the flower chart, starting with the buttercups and taking in order the line through the geraniums, first to the buckwheats and then to the mints, next the lines of development from the rose center, and finally the lily-orchid line. The detailed discussion of the value of the flower chart as to the effects of insects and wind upon the evolution of the flower, step by step, and its use as a key, is the subject of another book, "Flower Families and Ancestors."

There is a tendency among amateur botanists and flower lovers to shy at the scientific names of plants, but there is no doubt that the present state of inappropriateness and duplication in common names leads to uncertainty and confusion. Popular names have their value when pertinent or attractive, but it is necessary that they be supplemented by definite terms based upon accurate determination of structure and relationship. Experience has come to recognize the value of distinguishing plants by names made up of two parts or words, such as *Lilium canadense, Rosa californica, Coreopsis tinctoria,* etc. The first word refers to the *genus* and is always written with a capital. The second one indicates the *species* and is never capitalized in the latest usage. The meaning of the terms *genus* (plural *genera*) and of *species* (plural *species*) may be illustrated by the lilies and lupins. The tiger lily and the yellow lily belong to the *genus* of lilies, *Lilium,* but each has its own species designation, *tigrinum* and *parryi* respectively. The beach lupin, dwarf lupin and wand lupin are different kinds or species of the same genus, *Lupinus,* with the respective names of *chamissonis, nanus* and *formosus.* Genera that are related to each other are placed together in the same family, which always takes its name from that of a prominent genus belonging to it, and invariably ends in—*aceae,* the feminine plural of the Latin suffix,—*aceus,* meaning *like* or *related to. Rosaceæ,* for example, is the family of the roses, which includes not only the roses proper but also the cinquefoils, geums, spiræas, etc. The *Asteraceæ* or aster family comprises the asters, sunflowers, goldenrods, daisies, dandelions, dahlias, etc. The family name, *Asteraceæ,* is really an adjective agreeing with *plantæ,* plants, and meaning "plants related to the aster." The scientific name thus has a very definite and unmistakable application which is lacking in its translation, since in speaking of the asters, for instance, either the genus or the family may be meant. An attempt has been made in the text to specify as clearly as possible in those cases where confusion might arise.

BUTTERCUP FAMILY

RANUNCULACEÆ

Regardless of the bewildering variety shown by this family, its members can practically always be recognized by the large number of stamens and separate pistils, which are attached to the end of the stem at the same level with petals and sepals. The true buttercups, anemones, globe-flowers and peonies are all orthodox representatives with regular flowers, while columbines, larkspurs and monkshoods furnish a pleasing variation in their oddly shaped blossoms.

The genera of buttercups may be found scattered all over the world, but they show a preference for the temperate and cold portions of the northern hemisphere, especially in Europe. Many of them possess an acrid juice in stem and leaf that blisters the skin. This is so unusually caustic in a species of clematis that European beggars are said to use it purposely to produce sores in order to arouse sympathy and the ancients were accustomed to employ it in the removal of birthmarks and as a last recourse in cases of leprosy. Although this acrid juice is present in many of the buttercups and is even violently poisonous in some, in the majority it disappears under the influence of heat and certain species are safely eaten as pot-herbs in consequence. Others are useful as the source of dyes and drugs, but today the greatest value of this family lies in its contribution to the flower garden.

BUTTERCUP

RANUNCULUS CALIFORNICUS

(Plate 2, fig. 1)

From February to May, low grassy hills near the coast of California and southern Oregon are spread with a cloth of pale shining gold as the buttercup comes into bloom. The tall loosely branching stems sway in the breeze with slender grace, bearing near their

Plate 2

BUTTERCUP FAMILY

3
1
4
2
5

tips open clusters of many-petaled fragile blossoms that reflect the sunshine from polished surfaces. In spite of their beauty, they will prove a disappointment to anyone who gathers an armful, for the petals fall quickly and the charm of the bouquet is gone, even though the buds may continue to open after the stems have been placed in water.

The flowers of buttercups offer their pollen generously to all comers, but bees buzzing abroad in search of honey must seek diligently for the nectar hidden in glands at the base of the petals. As they tumble about busily, the pollen-laden anthers brush against their bodies and cover them with yellow powder. This they carry to other buttercups in quick succession, never satisfied until replete with honey and loaded with pollen. Some of the flowers are older, and instead of depositing pollen on the bee, they remove some that it already carries, for the group of pistils in their centers have sticky tips that come in contact with the powdery mass on legs and body.

The seeds of the California buttercup have been found useful by the Indians who parch them and grind them up into a flour that is eaten without further cooking. The bitter taste disappears under this treatment and the meal has the flavor of parched corn. The flowers also yield a considerable amount of early honey.

Buttercups are lovers of sunshine, and shunning the shadows of the woodlands, may be found in the drier soil of roadside and mountain meadow or in the mud of marsh and pond. It is to the fact that many of the commonest species haunt the home of the frog that they were given the name Ranunculus, for this is the Latin word for little frog. A pretty legend offers a more fanciful explanation. It is said that Ranunculus was a handsome Libyan youth with a beautiful voice, who dressed always in green and yellow silk and went about the countryside charming wood-nymphs and maidens with his melodies. On one occasion the poignant beauty of these affected him to such a degree that he expired in ecstasy. Orpheus, the god of music, took pity on the sweet singer and changed him into the little plant with yellow blossoms and green leaves, now known as Ranunculus.

Though scientists may puzzle their brains and disagree as to the probable origin of the buttercup, fairy-lore has no difficulty in offering several explanations. Another of these has to do with the rainbow-bridge built for Iris, the messenger of the gods, and with the pot of gold at the end of it. Many had tried and failed to find this treasure, but at last an old miser succeeded. As he hurried along with his bag full of round yellow gold-pieces, a mischievous little elf crept up behind and cut a hole in it. Unaware of his loss, the old man kept on his way, leaving a trail of shining disks in the grass. Fearful lest these disappear if they were not fastened to something, the fairies attached each to a flower stem and so the buttercups were born.

Other traditions have to do with the properties of the plants instead of their appearance and some of these connect the tall buttercup (Ranunculus acris) with various phases of insanity. In Pliny's writings reference is made to the "laughing leaves" of this species, which were said to produce excessive laughter and strange visions when brewed into a drink. The root was reputed a cure for insanity if gathered in the wane of the moon and hung about the neck in a linen cloth. In somewhat more modern times, the country-folk of England believed that the mere smell of the flowers produced madness.

Buttercups have long been cultivated, many of them doing well as aquatics or in moist corners of the rock garden, while others are suitable for borders. The great favorite is an Asiatic species (Ranunculus asiaticus) called the Persian buttercup and mentioned in literature as far back as 1629, but greatly improved since that time in both size and tint of the blossoms. These exhibit nearly every color except blue and some varieties are striped and variegated. The doubling of the petals may go so far as to produce flowers almost spherical in form and two inches in diameter, that are very unlike the familiar buttercup of field and meadow. The native buttercup makes a charming garden plant, growing readily from seed and producing an abundance of shining yellow blossoms from early February till late in the spring. It is not averse to moderate shade and may be grown in masses and rows or scattered among the grasses.

RED COLUMBINE

Aquilegia truncata

(Plate 2, fig. 2)

The brilliant red and yellow blossoms of the columbine swing at the tips of slender bending stems like gay butterflies on the wing. Unlike butterflies they shun the sunshine, and during spring and early summer, brighten the dusk of shady places with spots of vivid flame. To the casual observer the oddly formed flowers give no hint of their near kinship to the common yellow buttercup, nor even to larkspurs and monkshoods, but within the pendant blossom and well protected against sudden showers are the many stamens and separate pistils that are the insignia of the simplest flowers.

In preparing a feast of nectar the columbine is less extravagant than the meadow buttercup, but more generous than its other cousins the larkspur and monkshood, for it provides a nectary in each of the five spurs at the ends of the petals. Short-tongued bees find it impossible to sip the sweets in the usual way, so they often make use of the holes which enterprising bumble-bees have already bitten in the spurs, and follow their example by stealing the hidden store.

The red columbine grows in thickets and woodlands along the Pacific Coast as far north as Alaska and even ventures eastward to Montana and Utah. The eastern red columbine (Aquilegia canadensis) has smaller flowers of a less brilliant hue and prefers somewhat shadier situations. Colorado's state flower, the blue columbine (Aquilegia cœrulea), is very large, blue and white or occasionally creamy white, and often grows in dense masses in grassy openings of the spruce woods of the Rockies. The common garden columbine (Aquilegia vulgaris) has been brought over from its native haunts in Europe, and since it hybridizes readily, produces a great variety of forms and colors. Whether wild or naturalized, all species are well worth growing for the sake of the flowers in the early part of the season and the delicate foliage after the blooming is past.

The scientific name aquilegia is probably from the Latin word for eagle and refers to the fancied resemblance of the hooked spurs to eagle's talons. It has also been thought to come from a word meaning water-drawer in allusion to the spurs as funnels designed to hold water. The common name columbine is made from the Latin word for dove and likewise alludes to the spurred petals, but in this case they are seen to resemble a circle of doves with their heads close together over a dish of food.

Long well-known in heraldry, the columbine appears combined with the broom-flower on the arms of the Plantagenets and with the red rose as the emblem of the House of Lancaster. Throughout the Middle Ages various noblemen made use of both flower and foliage in various forms as decorations for crests, coats-of-arms or shields. Leaf and blossom offer a wealth of material for ornamental design, having been used as early as the fifteenth century in the border of an illumined manuscript, and by artists and decorators ever since. Poets have ever been wont to pay tribute to this charming flower, but though the earlier ones ascribe to it melancholy roles representing sorrow, desolation or ingratitude, recent writers pay less attention to its symbolism and sing the praises of its beauty.

There has been a movement afoot in this country to select the columbine as the national flower. Those who favor this candidate put forth the following reasons for their advocacy: it is native to nearly all the states in some form; it can easily be raised from seed in any garden; the name aquilegia associates it with the bird of freedom, our national eagle; and the name columbine suggests both Columbus and Columbia.

BLUE LARKSPUR

DELPHINIUM PARRYI

(Plate 2, fig. 3)

From April till June the wild-flowers of southern California fling a magic carpet of rainbow colors over hillside and mesa. Here and there in the mass of pink abronias, purple ice-plants, yellow evening-primroses and saffron cactus blossoms, the slender stalks of larkspur stand densely clustered with purple-blue flowers.

In the shade of the chaparral the stems reach a height of three feet and produce but a few unusually large flowers, while in dry sunny spots they are rarely over a foot high and the blossoms are crowded into a long spike.

It seems a far cry from the regular chalice of the yellow buttercup to the fanciful form of the blue larkspur, but hidden beneath the two drooping fringed petals is found the group of crowded stamens and three separate pistils to tell the story of near relationship. The other two petals, edged with white, also project over these parts and complete the protection against wetting by rain or dew. Their bases are snugly hidden away in the tip of the spur, in the form of two little sacks filled with honey. In trying to reach this store of sweets, bumble-bees blunder over the stamens that block the way and load themselves with pollen to be transported to another flower. Despite its abundance the larkspur is little inclined to waste the pollen. The anthers ripen by twos and fours instead of all at once and as their contents are shed and carried away, the filaments curve upward carrying the empty pollen-sacs out of the way and permitting fresh ones to take their places in the direct path of visitors. In the very center of the flower, three tiny vase-like pistils turn their tips so that the bees rarely fail to dust them with the golden powder when the stigmas are ready to receive it. Finally the tiny fruits swell, the sepals and petals of the blossom drop and it only remains for the pods to burst and scatter their seeds.

This blue larkspur is found in southern California in the chaparral and on grassy hillsides. It greatly resembles the tall larkspur (Delphinium exaltatum) of the East, which is dark-blue with yellow on the upper petals. There are other blue larkspurs throughout California and northward into Washington, which vary in the shade of blue and in minor features. In meadows and prairies east of the Rocky Mountains, there is a species (Delphinium azureum) of a delicate azure paling to white. There are many others growing wild in this country and all may be recognized by the peculiar shape of the upper sepal which has sufficient resemblance to the spur of a bird to suggest the popular name. The giver of the scientific name thought that the buds looked like dolphins as pictured in decorative art and so applied the Greek word delphinium, or little dolphin, to the plant.

A number of native larkspurs are poisonous to cattle, somewhat less so to horses and little if at all harmful to sheep. An extract made from the seeds of the field larkspur (Delphinium consolida) of Europe is poisonous if taken internally but is useful as an ointment or lotion.

Cultivated larkspurs afford a large number of beautiful forms and colors varying from white through all shades of blue, lavender and purple, pink and even yellow and scarlet. They may be single-flowered or very greatly doubled, perennial or annual, so that the range offered for individual choice is unusual. Besides being very ornamental in borders or groups because of their attractive foliage and luxuriant spikes of blossoms, they keep well when cut for bouquets or vases.

SCARLET LARKSPUR

DELPHINIUM CARDINALE

(Plate 2, fig. 4)

Like flaming torches scattered through the dry chaparral of early summer, the scarlet larkspur is startling in its vivid beauty. Blooming after the rains are over and when other flowers have mostly disappeared, its usual companions are tall yellow senecios, rose-colored live-forevers, creamy cactus and pale salvias. Whether surrounded by the dark-green or gray shrubs of the coastal sagebrush or standing solitary in broad river plains or stony streamways, the nearly leafless stems shoot up to a height of six feet or more and are tipped with long spikes of brilliant scarlet-vermilion blossoms.

Cool canyons of the Pacific Coast are the homes of another red larkspur (Delphinium nudicaule) which reflects the differences in its home environment by producing fewer flowers on shorter stems. The majestic height and brilliant coloring of the southern form, as well as the uniform flowering of the spikes, recommend it for wild gardens especially as these desirable features are fairly certain to become more and more marked under cultivation.

Larkspurs are especially attractive to bumble-bees and the nectar is so well protected by the spur which forms an extra covering for the honey-sacs, that smaller bees cannot bite through and steal it. Their tongues are far too short to reach it in the usual way so that bumble-bees are left in fairly complete possession. They find no difficulty in running their long tongues quickly into the spur while clinging to the lower sepals with their hind-legs and to the lateral ones with their fore-legs. So rapidly does the honey flow and so busily do the bumble-bees work that they are able to visit the same cluster of blossoms several times in succession. Red larkspurs also attract humming-birds, which are partial to this color, and their long bills are well adapted to extract nectar from the slender spurs.

MONKSHOOD

Aconitum columbianum

(Plate 2, fig. 5)

The slender spikes of monkshood stand straight and tall, like sentinels on guard among the grasses and herbs of moist mountain meadows. On shady brook-banks they stretch up to a height of six or eight feet and grow in closely clustered groups with other moisture-loving plants. Alders and maples form an arching canopy overhead and in their cool shadows, with roots reaching down towards the waters of the rushing brook, the dark blue-purple or white spikes of monkshood bloom through the summer.

The monkshood, like the columbine and larkspur, conceals its relationship to the buttercup under a fanciful disguise. It masquerades in a queer blue bonnet with floating ribbons instead of wearing a saucy dunce's cap as the larkspur does. Peeping beneath the hood, one half expects to see a tiny face, but finds instead the cluster of stamens and separate pistils so characteristic of the buttercup family.

The nectaries are snugly tucked away in the upper cowl-shaped sepal and take the form of tiny cornucopias on slender stalks. Long tongues are necessary to reach the honey and so dependent are monkshoods on bumble-bees for pollination that their very existence is at stake. It is a curious fact that countries such as New Zealand, Australia, Arabia and South Africa, which have no native bumble-bees also lack native monkshoods. The bee alights on the ribbon-like lower sepals, grasps the lateral ones with its front legs and as it sucks the nectar, moves its body back and forth over the stamens and stigmas. Besides helping itself to the honey so freely offered, it scrapes off the pollen clinging to head and body and packs it into pollen-baskets on its legs to be carried home and made into bread for the baby bees. Like its near relative the larkspur, the monkshood is careful of its store of pollen, not only protecting it against wetting but ripening the anthers by twos and fours and thus maintaining a constant supply for a week or more.

With the exception of southern California, this blue monkshood is found throughout the mountains of the West. There are several species in the Alleghenies that may also be quickly recognized by the peculiar helmet-shaped sepal. This is so characteristic that most of the common names have reference to it. In northern Europe the monkshood has sometimes been called Odin's helm, in allusion to the cap of invisibility supposed to form a part of his attire. More frequently it was Thor's hat, since the helmet-like shape was more suggestive of the god of war than of the god of wisdom. The resemblance was seen to be cowl-like when the Benedictine monks reached the Scandinavian countries, and the name monkshood resulted. To the Danes, it is Troll's hat or storm-hat.

The German name "devil's-root" alludes to the malign quality of the tuberous root, while the terms wolfsbane and wolfswort are somewhat more obscure in origin. One writer assumes that they refer to Thor's combat with the wolf and another that they are allusions to the practice which hunters have of putting the juice of the plant into raw meat in order to attract wolves to their destruction. This poison is so powerful that the natives of East India are said to use it on their arrows when hunting tigers, since even a slight wound will cause death in a short time. Armies of ancient times were also said to have indulged in a similar practice for the quick annihilation of their enemies.

It is the cultivated monkshood (Aconitum napellus) that furnishes the drug aconite which is used in medicine in various ways. Many of the wild species also are poisonous and cattle have been known to suffer from eating the plants when feed was scarce. Because of these dangerous qualities, monkshoods should never be planted near either the kitchen garden or the children's garden. Otherwise, they are attractive and satisfactory garden plants which produce ornamental foliage as well as flowers.

POPPY FAMILY

Papaveraceæ

Members of the poppy family resemble their close relatives the buttercups in possessing a large number of stamens, but they differ in the ovary, which shows the beginning of union in a one-celled capsule that splits into its original parts when ripe or even has partitions between them. Practically all poppies exude a milky juice when cut that may be yellow, white or red, but occasionally is merely watery or acrid. This is the source of the opium of commerce and of various medicinal drugs.

The poppies show a preference for the temperate and subtropical regions of the northern hemisphere but they may be found cultivated in all parts of the world. Of the latter, the choicest ornamentals are many of the true poppies, the California poppy, the Matilija poppy and the bleeding-heart.

The irregular flowers of the bleeding-heart and its closest relatives have lent warrant to their also being made into a separate family, but some of them resemble poppies so closely that it seems more desirable to indicate this relationship by placing them in the same family. They mark much the same advance upon the poppy flower plan that the monkshoods and larkspurs do over that of the regular buttercup.

Plate 3

POPPY FAMILY

1
2
3
4
5
6
7

CREAM-CUPS

Platystemon californicus

(Plate 3, fig. 1)

Strikingly like pale buttercups, the light-yellow blossoms of cream-cups flutter airily in the sea-breezes and spread a riot of spring bloom in the sandy soils of field and shore. They are often at their best on dunes where they are associated with pink abronias, yellow senecios, golden California poppies and baerias. Here the plants take on a robust form and sometimes reach a height of nine inches, with numerous hairy branching stems and many flowers. In the adobe soil of cliffs, however, where water is harder to get than from loose sand, the entire plant becomes dwarfed, with but a few stems two or three inches high, tiny blossoms and small leaves only at the base. When in the shade of shrubs or overtopped by other herbs, the stems grow towards the light to a height of fifteen inches or more and are thin-leaved and sparsely hairy, with larger flowers. Usually the blossoms are a pale straw-color or creamy white and the petals are cupped, so that the common name is not only a pretty one, but appropriate as well. Sometimes each petal may bear a darker yellow spot at the base or tip, or the entire petal take on deeper yellow tints, and occasionally a rare form with maroon-red flowers can be found. The oddly flattened stamens in all are directly referred to in the scientific name, platystemon.

Although cream-cups are placed in the same group with the poppies, they actually occupy the borderland between these and buttercups, sharing the features of both. Like some buttercups they have six to nine petals instead of the four so characteristic of poppies. Both families usually possess numerous stamens and many pistils, but in the poppies the latter have become more or less united into a single many-chambered structure. The number of pistils in cream-cups varies from six to twenty and these are united at first but separate at maturity. As in the other poppies, the sepals fall as the bud opens, but unlike them there are three instead of two.

WIND POPPY

Papaver californicum

(Plate 3, fig. 2)

The vermilion-red disks of the wind poppy glow here and there like bright flecks of flame in the shelter of the chaparral or in shady dells. They bloom throughout the spring in central and southern California, but are so fragile that the petals fall at a touch. Unfortunately, the seeker after wild-flowers may not know this and many a delicate beauty has been plucked only to be at once thrown aside.

The flaming poppy (Papaver heterophyllum) may be found side by side with its twin sister and is practically indistinguishable from it. Close inspection will reveal the fact that the ovary is crowned by a short slender style and that the juice is yellow instead of milky. Instead of dressing exactly alike, the one ornaments its scarlet petals with a green spot at the base of each, while the other shows a preference for crimson.

The seeds of both the wind poppy and the flaming poppy may easily be obtained and should be sown in shady or partly shady spots in the garden. The Shirley poppy is greatly prized in this country as an ornamental although the blossoms are short-lived. This variety is derived from the corn poppy (Papaver rhœas) of Europe which runs wild through the wheat-fields and gives the farmer a deal of trouble. Nevertheless, the scarlet blossoms scattered through the golden wheat in company with the blue cornflower make a beautiful picture in the landscape. The Iceland poppy (Papaver nudicaule) is another variety suitable for cultivation but it never attains the brilliant scarlet of the Shirley poppy although offering a greater range of color, from white through yellow, orange and certain shades of red. The crumpled satiny petals are very attractive and the flowers are excellent for cutting. Running a close second in the competition for favor, the oriental poppy (Papaver orientale) produces the largest flowers of all. These were originally scarlet with a black spot at the base of each petal, but now vary through several shades of red to orange, salmon and pale-pink. The opium poppy (Papaver somniferum) is also frequently grown in gardens for its many-colored blossoms with petals which are variously doubled and fringed under cultivation but drop quickly when the flowers are gathered.

The common name poppy is merely a corrupt form of papaver and this is connected with the word pap, formerly used to designate a thickened milk fed to infants. The milky juice of poppies, however, is poisonous and children especially should be warned against tasting or chewing any part of a poppy plant even though the seeds happen to be harmless. These are used by Europeans, in cakes and cookies; they also yield an oil that is used in cooking as a substitute for olive oil and in painting as a drier. Opium is obtained from the juice of the opium poppy and is valued by Orientals especially as an intoxicant, although its continued use results in complete physical and moral degradation. Of the twenty different alkaloids which opium contains, but one is used in medicine as morphine for relieving pain and inducing sleep.

Since sleep has often been used in a figurative sense for death, the poppy flower has long been recognized as a symbol for the latter. In mythology, Somnus, the god of sleep, was always represented as crowned with or surrounded by poppy flowers. A legend relates that this god created the poppy in order to soothe Ceres when distracted over the loss of her daughter Proserpina. The grief of the goddess led her to neglect the growing crops which were her especial care, and they were about to perish, when the drink distilled by Somnus from the seeds of the poppy caused her to fall into a deep sleep, during which she became refreshed and the vegetation revived. Since then the goddess of the harvest is represented as wearing a garland of poppies mingled with wheat, and poppy seeds were offered to her when the prosperity of the crops was especially desired.

The young men and maidens of Greece and Rome were accustomed to put the sincerity of their loves to the test by a little ceremony with poppy petals, and to this day the peasant girls of Switzerland have the same custom. A petal of the poppy flower is placed in the left hand and struck quickly with the right. If nothing happens, love is failing, but if the petal bursts with a popping sound like that of a kiss, it signifies that the lover remains constant to his sweetheart.

CALIFORNIA POPPY

Eschscholtzia californica

(Plate 3, fig. 3)

Magic carpets of gold are flung far and wide over hillside and valley as the California poppy comes into bloom. At the height of its glory in the spring, when the winter rains have been seasonable and sufficient, the blossoms may cover many square miles so thickly as to be visible at great distances. One poppy bed, twenty miles long by ten wide, has been seen as a sheet of yellow from a peak forty miles away. Another, composed entirely of the orange-red variety, was of such brilliant hue and of such unbroken extent as to look from afar like the bare red earth of a great Permian exposure.

The California poppy is exceedingly variable in all its parts. The color may range from white, turning to pink with age, through all shades of yellow, from pale-lemon to pure canary and deep orange-red. Some forms have contrasting spots of color at the base of the petals, or gradual shadings from paler to deeper tints. On the sea-shore the plants send up stems but a few inches tall from a close rosette of leaves and bear a small number of large flowers. In more open spots they may be much larger, more branched and flowery. In competition with grasses and other herbs on the hillsides, there is often but one slender stem bearing a single blossom at its tip.

The various forms are sometimes named as different varieties or even species. They are at home everywhere along the coast and in interior valleys throughout California, northward to Oregon and Washington, south into Mexico, across the Colorado Desert and Arizona and eastward into New Mexico.

The beauty of form and color of the satin-petaled blossoms, as well as the delicate charm of its gray-green finely cut foliage, make this state flower of California a prime favorite with nature lovers and home gardeners everywhere that it is known. It blooms profusely under cultivation and when the cut flowers are placed in water, they open and close for several days before finally dropping their petals. There is no distinct fragrance, but the fresh smell of the flowers is suggestive of the open country.

An alert attention is necessary to discover the sepals of the California poppy as they enclose the bud in the form of a tiny peaked pale-yellow cap, which is pushed off and falls to the ground as the bud expands. The blossoms of the "drowsy one," as it is sometimes called in Spanish, open in the waxing sunshine of the morning, though on cool days they are laggards, waking up only at noon. When it is chill or foggy they apparently decide that it really is not worth while getting up at all, and so remain tightly coiled until the sun comes again. The petals begin to close as the shadows lengthen and are usually rolled together long before sunset, folding about each other again just as in the bud, but not so tightly.

The outer row of anthers starts to crack as the flower unfolds and by noon others follow as the first ones move downward and out of the way. On the second day the stigmas bend toward the center of the flower to receive their load of pollen, but the actual loading is usually done on the day following. A day or two later the petals and stamens fall, exposing the broad reddish disk which bears a young seed-pod capped by the yellow style.

None of the various alkaloids to be found in the California poppy are commercially of any worth. However, the plants furnish valuable winter forage for cattle on ranges of the Southwest, and broad fields of yellow blossoms disappear quickly in satisfying bovine appetites.

In realms of art, both flowers and foliage furnish a wealth of material, though the satiny sheen of the petals may be the despair of the colorist. An Indian legend ascribes the presence of gold in the earth to the fallen petals of this poppy as they drop year after year and sink into the soil.

BUSH-POPPY

Dendromecon rigida

(Plate 3, fig. 4)

With its wealth of large bright-yellow flowers and grayish-green foliage, the bush-poppy lends a sunny look to the landscape even on cloudy days. It is especially fond of burned-over ground which it often occupies quickly and completely, though as a rule only scattered individuals occur here and there among the shrubs of the chaparral of southern and middle California.

Poppies are known as pollen-flowers, since they have no nectar and rely on an abundance of the golden powder to attract their insect friends. The flowers of the bush-poppy have a fresh smell like that of cucumbers but are ornamental only if left undisturbed, for the petals fall soon after the blossoms are gathered. This habit of all poppies has been immortalized by Robert Burns, who in his poetry compares the nature of pleasures to the evânescence of the blossoms when picked.

The word dendromecon is derived from the Greek, meaning tree and poppy, but the name tree-poppy, frequently used for this species, is not strictly applicable, since the shrubs are rarely taller than ten feet and are bushy in outline. The seeds are difficult to germinate and so can scarcely be recommended for home cultivation. A near relative, the Matilija-poppy (Romneya coulteri), is one of the most magnificent shrubs that grows wild anywhere. Its diaphanous blossoms, with clusters of golden stamens and crinkly white petals, are from five to nine inches in diameter and very abundant on the tall stems. The prickly-poppy (Argemone platyceras) bears similar though smaller flowers but is not shrubby and is often called thistle-poppy because of its prickly grayish-green foliage so like that of a thistle.

PINK DICENTRA

Dicentra formosa

(Plate 3, fig. 5)

The pale waxen flowers of the pink dicentra hang pendant from curving stems here and there in the shadows of moist woods.

The diligent seeker for shy blossoms may find these through the summer in favored spots of the Coast Ranges and in the Sierra Nevada up to 9,000 feet. They are especially large and showy in Paradise Valley, but in the Yosemite may be easily overlooked since the plants seldom flower there. The delicate gray-green leaves, beautifully cut into a graceful fringe, are unusually attractive, and the blossoms, although they are somewhat smaller and paler, closely resemble those of the bleeding-heart (Dicentra spectabilis) of old-fashioned gardens. Some species are much less heart-shaped than others, two of the petals forming spur-like projections which contain the nectar. It is this form that has suggested the name dicentra, which means two-spur. This peculiar shape excludes most visitors from the honey which is stored at the base of the petals. Few have tongues long enough to reach it, but some bumble-bees use their strong jaws to bite holes and steal it, while smaller bees make use of these later to secure their share.

A dicentra of the East is called Dutchman's-breeches (Dicentra cucullaria) and, though the dainty blossoms are white or pale-pink, their two petals baggy at one end and tapering to two narrow extensions look very like this picturesque apparel hung upside down on a clothes-line. This is one of the earliest harbingers of spring in the woods of New England and westward to the Missouri. Only recently has this charming plant been found to be dangerously poisonous to stock, although long known in certain localities as stagger-weed. Another common eastern relative has white flowers flushed with pink at the tips of the spurs and is called squirrel-corn (Dicentra canadensis) because of its many small tubers. All respond readily to cultivation in rich light soil and some degree of shade, such as they are accustomed to in their native haunts. They are perennials and the dainty blossoms and graceful foliage make a combination of unusual beauty.

GOLDEN EARDROPS

Dicentra chrysantha

(Plate 3, fig. 6)

The tall stems of this yellow dicentra bear aloft loose clusters of golden blossoms that perch jauntily erect instead of drooping like other bleeding-hearts or like the golden eardrops they are assumed to resemble. In contrast to the stiff stems, which are often five feet tall, the finely cut leaves, a foot or more long, and pale shining green, seem unusually graceful.

The plants are not very abundant but may be found scattered here and there among the wild buckwheat and salvias of the plains and lower foothills in southern California. Though not often grown in the wild garden, they should be very effective placed here and there among low herbs or grouped in the background. A rarer species (Dicentra ochroleuca) occurs occasionally in chaparral burns in the mountains, where it grows sometimes as tall as ten feet, with beautiful fern-like leaves three feet long. The flowers—pale straw-color with purple tips on the inner petals—are clustered at the ends of the stems in panicles sometimes two or three feet long. Altogether, this species in favorable situations is as striking as it is rare and quite different in appearance from its delicate woodland relatives.

GOLDEN CORYDALIS

Corydalis aurea

(Plate 3, fig. 7)

A lover of the open spaces, the golden corydalis covers gravelly soils with masses of feathery foliage and open clusters of bright-yellow blossoms on delicate stems. When moisture is lacking the plants may become dwarfed to an inch or two in height, but where conditions permit luxuriant growth a single plant may be a foot tall and cover an area two feet across. The genus is closely related to the bleeding-heart and Dutchman's-breeches, but it has a single spur and the flowers are yellow instead of pink. The earliest blossoms appear in March while laggards may be found in the mountains in late summer and early autumn.

The name corydalis is derived from the Greek words for crested-lark and refers to the single spur of the flower. The difficulty of getting at the store of honey in the slender curved sack tempts short-tongued bees to robbery although the blossoms have honest pollinators also. The name of fumitory, sometimes applied to this genus, is derived from the Latin word for smoke since the odor of the bruised foliage is quite like that of smoke. Pliny ascribes the origin of the term to the fact that when the leaves are rubbed on the eyes they cause smarting tears just as smoke does, while earlier writers speak of the curious belief that the plant was produced without seeds from "vapours arising out of the earth."

All the species of Corydalis are easy of cultivation and will grow in half-shade although they prefer full sunlight. Some are showy purple or rose-color (Corydalis bulbosa, C. alleni) while others have a spur an inch long (Corydalis nobilis). Several have been used in medicine as tonics or as remedies in chronic skin diseases.

CAPER FAMILY

Capparidaceæ

The capers are very close relatives of the mustards and might even be regarded as their direct ancestors. They are to be distinguished by the numerous projecting stamens and by the fact that the flowers lack the typical form of the mustard blossom. The members of this family are equally at home in the Old World and the New and are distributed fairly uniformly over the tropical and sub-tropical portions of both hemispheres.

It is a species from the Mediterranean region that furnishes the French capers whose pungent flavor is considered an indispensable adjunct to some sauces and salads. The Rocky Mountain bee-plant adds its quota to the dinner-table in the form of a very excellent honey. This is a wild-flower of the West and all summer long fields and roadsides are redeemed by the clusters of beautiful rose-purple blossoms massed on tall plants. The only ornamental caper of any repute is another species of Cleome, known as the giant spider-plant and grown for its odd flowers. These are rose-purple or white, with blue or purple stamens, and both petals and stamens are so long and sprawling as to give the effect noted in the name.

Plate 4

CAPER FAMILY

MUSTARD FAMILY

VIOLET FAMILY

MILKWORT FAMILY

8
3
2
1
6
5
4
7

BLADDER-POD

Isomeris arborea

(Plate 4, fig. 1)

The low shrubs of the bladder-pod, with smooth green leaves and loose clusters of yellow flowers, contrast attractively with the uniform gray of the coastal sagebrush covering hills and cliffs in southern California. Though the blossoms themselves are not ill-smelling, the bruised foliage has a strongly pungent odor that is distinctly unpleasant. A prominent characteristic of the plants is the large leathery pods which droop on long stalks and contain two rows of bitter pea-like seeds. The name refers to these fruits which are not only bladder-like in shape but also filled with air so that they crack with a popping sound if crushed when ripe.

MUSTARD FAMILY

Brassicaceæ

The mustard family is an exceedingly large and useful one with members scattered all over the world. Some of these reach the limits of conditions in which flowering plants can grow, in the polar regions and on the highest mountains, but the majority are to be found in the south of Europe and Asia Minor. Many are familiar occupants of both flower and vegetable gardens. Of the former, perhaps the best-known are sweet-alyssum, candytuft, and rocket; of the latter, the cabbage and its varieties, kale, cauliflower, broccoli, and brussels-sprouts, are the most important. Together with turnips and radishes they add vitamines and bulk to the daily diet while horse-radish, mustard, garden-cress and water-cress play their parts as condiments or spurs to the jaded appetite. Of less well-known but interesting foreigners, should be mentioned the woad and the rose-of-Jericho. The leaves of the former yield a blue dye which was used by the Picts and Scots for painting their bodies. Since that time blue has remained the national color for the robes of royalty. The rose-of-Jericho, or resurrection plant, lives in the sandy deserts of Syria and Algeria and is far-famed for its ability to revive when placed in water, even when completely dried out and apparently dead.

The mustard flower is made up of four sepals and four petals which are arranged like the four parts of a Maltese cross and the family itself was formerly called Cruciferæ, which means cross-bearing. Today, however, it is more familiarly known by the name of a prominent genus. It is this form of the mustard blossom that distinguishes it at a glance from that of the closely allied capers, as well as the fact that the stamens are either four or six in number and of these, two are always shorter. Finally, the ovary of the mustards is two-celled and lacks the stalk on which the pistil of the capers is borne.

WESTERN WALL-FLOWER

Erysimum asperum

(Plate 4, fig. 2)

The chief charm of the western wall-flower lies in the range of lovely color exhibited by its globe-like clusters of flowers. This runs the gamut from a clear lemon-color through canary and golden-yellow to bright-orange or deep burnt-orange. An additional attraction is a delightful fragrance which lures honey-seeking bees to the nectar at the base of the petals.

The cream-colored wall-flower (Erysimum grandiflorum) of the sea-shore is paler even than the most lightly tinted inland specimens and presents a striking contrast to the darkest shades. It is to be found along the coast from southern California to Oregon, and is so fond of sandy soil as to grow on the dunes themselves. Both species of wall-flower are readily cultivated and deserve their places in the garden beside their better-known relatives.

The name erysimum is from the Greek word meaning to draw blisters and probably refers to the early use of the acrid juice for this purpose. Even today the name blister-cress is sometimes applied to the plant.

The common wall-flower (Cheiranthus cheiri), which is a favorite spring bloomer in Old World gardens, has a long history of flower-lore and romantic associations woven about it. When running wild, it sends its roots into the cracks and crevices of crumbling castle walls and battlements. Stone churches and monuments, monasteries and towers that have fallen into decay are the chosen haunts of this cheery plant which has thus won the name of wall-flower and has come to be regarded as an emblem of fidelity in misfortune. Our western wall-flower has little opportunity to become a romantic feature of moonlit ruins in California but is content to strike root in the dry soil of plains or openings in the chaparral. It is a ready traveler and has taken up homestead claims throughout the West, venturing north into British Columbia, south to Mexico and east as far as Texas, Arkansas and Minnesota.

WILD RADISH

Raphanus sativus

(Plate 4, fig. 3)

Attractive as the succulent red or white roots of the garden-radish may look on the dinner-table, they are rarely associated with the flower in the mind of the consumer, but when this household favorite escapes from cultivation, it takes to the open with a profusion of bloom that transforms fields and vacant lots. The blossoms are beautifully colored, from white with rose-purple veinings, through delicate-pink to dark rose-purple, and all exhibit in marked degree the typical cross-shaped arrangement of the petals.

The ease with which the seed germinates gave rise to the name raphanus, which means to appear quickly, while radish is from the Latin word for root. The peoples of Temperate Asia fully appreciated its value as a succulent vegetable, for there are records of its use over two thousand years ago, but modern methods of cultivation have produced a great variety of forms not in existence in the early days. Some of the Chinese and Japanese radishes are huge plants with roots that may weigh forty or fifty pounds and are used as a cooked vegetable. Quite different in appearance is another Chinese variety which, with a diameter of only an inch, sometimes reaches the length of a foot or so. The edible part of the rat-tailed or serpent radish (Raphanus caudatus) consists of the pods which are a foot or more long, slender and curiously bent or curved. They may be pickled as well as eaten raw, and though rarely grown in this country are well worth attention as a curiosity.

The black mustard (Brassica nigra), a close relative of the radishes, is a beautiful sight in California during the spring and early summer when the fragrant blossoms cover hillsides and valleys with a smother of pale-yellow. It is the tiny seeds that furnish the useful plasters and other household remedies and for the sake of which the plants are cultivated. Escaping from cultivation, they spread rapidly and early settlers say that formerly thousands of acres were covered with such dense thickets of tall mustard plants that it was necessary to warn school-children against the dangers of getting lost in them.

VIOLET FAMILY

VIOLACEÆ

The violet family is a small one, with its herbaceous species principally native to the northern hemisphere and the woody ones to the equatorial region of America. The underground parts of a number yield a substance with emetic and laxative properties, while the fragrant oil distilled from the petals appears in exquisite perfumes. The flowers are always irregular in shape, with five sepals, five petals, five stamens and a one-celled ovary which generally splits into three parts when ripe.

The popular violets of our East all have blue flowers which are borne on slender leafless stalks. The butterfly violet loves the borders of woodlands and thickets and the birds-foot violets lend a blue tinge to meadow and prairie in the height of spring. They are the most flowery of all, the leaves often being smothered in a mass of blossoms.

The nectar-bearing spur of the violets suggests the attraction they once held for bees as do also the various guide-lines and markings on the lower petal. Although some species are still pollinated by insects, the great majority rely upon a method of self-pollination that is peculiar to this type of flower. Towards the end of the flowering season, the plants put forth fewer and fewer gaily colored blossoms, and instead of opening, the buds remain closed or even buried in the leaf-mold and earth at the base of the plants. Within this bud the transfer of pollen is made directly from the anthers to the pistil. As the fruit matures it splits into three little canoe-shaped sections, each filled with a row of shining brown seeds. As the segments dry, the sides pinch together and the seeds are flung in all directions to distances of several feet. In some parts of England the country-folk believe that the violet breeds fleas. Since the seeds are about the size and color of this lively insect, their brisk jumping about through the air when thrust from the capsule, furnishes sufficient warrant for the belief.

YELLOW VIOLET

VIOLA GLABELLA

(Plate 4, fig. 4)

Inconspicuous amid the luxuriant growth of woodlands, this small yellow violet, with smooth thin leaves, well merits the terms shy and modest so often applied to violets. It is not abundant although widely distributed in the moist woods of the Coast Ranges and Sierra Nevada from central California to Alaska and Alberta. The yellow violet (Viola pubescens) of eastern woods also has a leafy stem and loves the shade. Both species are more sparing of their flowers than are the blue violets and only a few bloom at a time.

WHITE VIOLET

VIOLA BLANDA

(Plate 4, fig. 5)

Boggy meadows and cold springs in the mountains are the favorite haunts of this tiny fragrant white violet so faintly tinged with blue-lavender. It is said that all violets were originally white, but once upon a time Venus stepped upon a sharp thorn and the drops of blood issuing from the wound dyed the petals purple. This color is so typical as to be designated by the name of the flower itself. The blue violets are held to symbolize constancy or fidelity while the white violet is thought to stand for innocence and modesty.

Although nowhere abundant, the white violet ranges widely in mountain valleys from the Sierra Nevada to Alaska and eastward to the Rockies and Atlantic. The white violet (Viola canadensis) that is found in northern and eastern woods is considerably larger than this western one and differs also in having a yellow center and a violet or purple tinge on the outer side of the petals.

PURPLE VIOLET

VIOLA CANINA

(Plate 4, fig. 6)

Royal in coloring, famed in legend and poetry, the woodland violet hides shyly among the grasses of moist mountain meadows and conceals its blossoms beneath broad leaves of pale-green. This small purple violet of deepest hue may be found in wet meadows and swampy places of the northern hemisphere the world over. In southern California it seeks half-bogs or the shade of shrubs near the coast and that of pines and tall grasses in the Tuolumne Meadows of the Yosemite.

So lovely a flower as the violet could scarcely escape attention from the earliest times, and although the word viola is the Latin name of the flower, there is a legend that derives it from the nymph Io, who was transformed into a heifer by Jupiter on the approach of his jealous wife. Violets are also referred to frequently in the classics and they were especially prized by the Athenians who cultivated them throughout the year and wove them into chaplets and garlands, besides offering a golden violet to the winner of certain floral games. In later days the violet was adopted as the emblem of the Bonapartists, and Napoleon's followers wore rings and watch-ribbons of violet-color during his exile and upon his return welcomed him with violets. As a consequence these flowers were so identified with Napoleon that it was dangerous to wear them after the Battle of Waterloo. Somewhat later, however, they became the badge of the Liberal Party in Paris. In North America four states have chosen the violet as the official flower.

Side by side in the garden the fragrant sweet-violet hiding beneath a wealth of foliage offers a striking contrast to the upstanding pansies looking up with such anxious little faces. To be sure, the pansy (Viola tricolor) has had the benefit of intensive culture at the hands of the florist, and starting in Europe as a simple tricolored flower of the fields, emerges finally as the result of much crossing and selection. In its velvet petals, lovely and varied colors and large size, it is as far removed from its wild-flower ancestor as the present-day daughter of an English earl may be from her country-bred forebears.

PANSY VIOLET

VIOLA PEDUNCULATA

(Plate 4, fig. 7)

The bright-golden flowers of the pansy violet smile cheerily on the hillsides of southern California through March and April. Unlike their woodland sisters that hang their heads in the shadows, they seek the sunshine, and when growing in the shade of the chaparral stretch up towards the light sometimes to a height of two feet. Where there is plenty of room and moisture in bare sandy spots, leafy rosettes appear at short intervals along the runners and soon carpet the ground. If the seed germinates where the soil is too dry for luxuriant growth, the plants become stunted, as do all living things that are under-nourished, and bear only small flowers on stems two or three inches tall.

The sprightly wide-awake look of the blossoms gives point to the name of Johnny-jump-up which is sometimes used, and explains the adoption of this species as the emblem of rural happiness. Its fresh woodsy odor is very pleasant and adds to the attractiveness of the plants as garden perennials.

MILKWORT FAMILY

POLYGALACEÆ

The polygala family is so odd that no one seems to know very definitely just what its relationship to other families is. The flowers have shared the experience of those of several other groups, resembling each in some ways and differing in others. It is a small family with most of its genera to be found in the tropical and warm southern temperate zones, although the type genus, Polygala, has its representatives all over the globe. Some possess substances that are tonic, astringent or emetic and have been assumed to be specific for various troubles, from lung diseases to snake-bites.

The flowers are irregular in shape and consist of five sepals, two of which are colored like petals, three or five petals, and stamens twice the number of the petals. The ovary is two-celled and the fruit a fleshy capsule.

MILKWORT

POLYGALA CALIFORNICA

(Plate 4, fig. 8)

The dainty little plants of the milkwort with their queerly shaped rose-purple blossoms seek the shade or peep forth from the edges of woodlands on the hills of the Coast Ranges. The flowers may easily be mistaken for pea-blossoms or near relatives at least, since they too have wings and a keel. The standard, however, is lacking, and close inspection will reveal other differences. The two broad wings are brightly colored sepals which enclose the three inconspicuous petals. One of the latter is curiously fringed and thus affords the bee a foothold as it probes for the nectar. The entire method of pollination is intricate and unusual, but the flowers are not entirely dependent upon insect visitors. Like the violets, the milkwort bears inconspicuous blossoms near the roots, which do not take the trouble to open at all. They are self-pollinated in the bud and open only when the seeds are ripe.

Long ago it was thought that cows fed upon milkwort produced more milk than usual, and so the name polygala was fashioned from the Greek for much milk.

MALLOW FAMILY

MALVACEÆ

Mallows are primarily inhabitants of the tropics and they diminish in number with distance from the equator. There are more of them, however, in the northern tropics, and also more in America than in the Old World. Their main contributions to commerce consist in the mucilage-like substance present in many of the species and in the fibres produced by others. The former is useful as an emollient and was originally the foundation of marshmallow candy, but this is now obtained from other sources. The most famous member of the mallow family is the cotton-plant, which was first cultivated in India over two thousand years ago and today clothes the whole world with garments made from the soft hairs of the seed coats. The seeds themselves yield an oil used for burning and in the manufacture of soap, while the residue left after extraction is pressed into cotton-seed cakes as feed for cattle.

Other contributions made by members of this family are acids for refreshing drinks, drugs, a perfume, the baobab fruit so popular with the negroes, and okra used in the South as a vegetable and thickening for soups. The Chinese secure the black coloring matter which they use on their hair and shoes, from the flowers of a species of Hibiscus. There are two interesting and ornamental East Indian species of this genus, one of which has been introduced into our East and runs wild there. It is termed flower-of-an-hour on account of its opening for a brief period of sunshine each day. The other is called the "changeable-rose," because it turns from white to rose-color and finally to purple in the space of one day in East India, but in cooler climates this transformation may require a week.

The mallows occupy a position on the family-tree in the direct line of descent between buttercups and geraniums. They resemble both the buttercups and poppies in the large number of stamens, but these are united by their filaments into a characteristic column. The parts of the ovary are so lightly joined together that they split apart easily when ripe and illustrate the intermediate stage between the separate pistils of the buttercups and the compound ovary of the geraniums.

Plate 5

MALLOW FAMILY

GERANIUM FAMILY

FLAX FAMILY

1
2
3
4
5
6
7

BUSH-MALLOW

Malvastrum fasciculatum

(Plate 5, fig. 1)

The delicate rose-lavender flowers of the bush-mallow, set among soft gray-green leaves on wand-like branches, make the tall shrubs a distinctive feature of hillsides and canyons in southern California. The fragrant blossoms appear during spring and summer, and look very like small hollyhocks. The dark-crimson of the stamens forms a pleasing contrast to the paler petals, their number and habit of uniting the filaments into a column furnishing a clue to their relationship.

Near relatives of the bush-mallow that are favorites in garden and greenhouse are the hollyhock ranking first, with abutilon and hibiscus not quite so well known. The tree mallow (Malvaviscus arboreus) is attractive not only because of its beauty but also on account of its ease of growth and freedom from insects. Of native mallows, the red-flowered species (Malvastrum coccineum) is spread widely over the Great Plains, where its vermilion blossoms furnish a striking note of color to extensive areas. The round-leaved mallow (Malva rotundifolia) bears inconspicuous pale flowers and abundant foliage, its popularity being due to the mealy fruits that children know as "cheeses."

The name malvastrum means mallow-like and the word mallow is connected with the Greek for soft, since some members of the family possess a mucilaginous substance used in poultices.

MISSION-MALLOW

Lavatera assurgentiflora

(Plate 5, fig. 2)

The brilliant rose-purple flowers with conspicuous dark veinings, together with the beautiful maple-like evergreen leaves of the mission-mallow, amply justified the Franciscan monks in their choice of this shrub as an ornamental in their gardens. From these it has escaped and now runs wild throughout the coast region of California, though found most abundantly in the northern part of the state. It is especially striking in the ravines and gullies of bold headlands, where it braves the salt spray in company with the silvery saltbush. For this reason it is often employed as a windbreak for vegetable gardens near the sea. The plants are easy of cultivation, and will grow from seed to a height of six feet and flower within the year. They stand drouth well and make an interesting hedge when closely planted.

CHECKERBLOOM

Sidalcea malvæflora

(Plate 5, fig. 3)

The spreading stems of the checkerbloom rise gracefully from basal clusters of geranium-like leaves and bear exquisite rose-lavender flowers along their upper sides. Found along the coast as far north as Washington and eastward to Wyoming and Texas, they form an attractive feature of grassy hills and mesas in springtime and furnish an effective contrast to the stiff bunches of grass-irises.

The blossoms open in the sunshine, when they are eagerly sought by bees for their wealth of pollen and in some measure for their nectar also. They close in the late afternoon of sunshiny days, but on cloudy ones do not open at all.

GERANIUM FAMILY

Geraniaceæ

The limits of this large and attractive family are variable, but are here considered to include not only the geraniums proper but the closely allied balsams, tropæolums and wood-sorrels. The first group is widely distributed in both the Old and New Worlds, with a preference for the warmer parts. Some yield astringents and others a sweet volatile oil that is used as an adulterant of essence of roses. Geranium oil possesses an attraction for certain insects, parasitic on forest trees in Japan, and is used as a lure so that the pests can be collected and destroyed. In South Africa there grows a member of the geranium family with a resinous stem, which burns with a flame and is used by the natives as a torch.

The familiar house and garden plant that is popularly called geranium belongs to a different genus, Pelargonium, and is listed under this name in seed catalogs and at flower shows, where it appears in a large number of beautiful and striking varieties. The flowers are many of them quite irregular in form, and of these the ivy-geranium trails over the ground or walls and produces a wealth of bloom in California. The rose-geranium is also a favorite, especially on account of its fragrant leaves. The balsams too have irregular blossoms with a spurred sepal. They are natives of India and Africa, where they prefer the mountainous regions. The familiar garden-balsam is originally from East India, but today may be found cultivated around the world. It has pods similar to those of the wild touch-me-not, which snap open at a touch and send the ripe seeds in all directions. The wild species are often called jewelweed because the "bloom" of the leaves causes raindrops or dewdrops on them to sparkle like diamonds.

The tropæolums, which are commonly known as nasturtiums, form another group with irregular flowers. They are natives of South America, chiefly of the western slopes of the Andes, but make themselves very much at home in gardens of California, from which they escape and run riot with a profusion of bloom that is amazing. The buds and young fruits of some of the species are pickled and eaten as a relish abroad, and use is also made of flowers, leaves and stems in this country as an addition to salads and sandwiches. A species in Peru possesses farinaceous roots that enter into the composition of a sort of jelly relished by the natives.

The wood-sorrels resemble geraniums proper in the regularity of the flower and the number of its parts, but the capsule has many seeds and lacks the long beak. The leaves too are very different, being made up of three leaflets, which respond to low temperatures by folding together and going to sleep. The cultivated species have been brought from South Africa and tropical America; their flowers are mostly large and showy, with a preference for yellow or rose-purple.

WILD GERANIUM

Geranium incisum

(Plate 5, fig. 4)

The wild geranium brightens the margins of the Sierra woods with magenta-colored blossoms or ventures forth along the roadsides. It is a familiar sight in spring and summer, from the Yosemite northward, and eastward to the Rockies. The shade forms are taller, smoother and thinner-leaved than are the plants that prefer the sunshine, the latter often being much dwarfed in dry situations.

White-flowered forms may be confused with a related species (Geranium richardsoni), which grows in the same general region as well as in the Rocky Mountains, while the pink geranium (Geranium cæspitosum) of the latter locality can be distinguished only by the specialist. All these may well be considered the same species. The eastern wild geranium (Geranium maculatum) finds its home in open deciduous woods from Canada to the Gulf of Mexico and from the Mississippi to the Atlantic. Its root furnishes the extract of geranium used in medicine as an astringent.

Small bees, honey-bees and bumble-bees are all fond of the nectar of the wild geranium and hover about continually on bright days. The honey collects at the base of the petals and the insects often touch the pollen-laden anthers as they hasten from one nectary to the next one. There are two groups of anthers of five each, the upper row somewhat longer than the lower one. The stigmas remain closed while the longer stamens are shedding pollen and until the shorter ones mature. When the pollen is practically all gone and the anthers have begun to drop from their filaments, the stigmas curl back and are ready to receive the pollen brought from other flowers.

Several members of the geranium family are commonly known by terms descriptive of the seed-vessel. Geranium itself is from the Greek for crane and is therefore frequently known as cranes-bill, while pelargonium means storks-bill and the well-known filaree or erodium herons-bill. In all, the pod is long, slender and sharp, suggestive of the bill of these long-legged waders.

When the capsule of the geranium is ripe, the five sections split apart, the slender attachments giving each the form of a sling. These recoil suddenly as they dry and the seeds are shot to some distance from the parent plant. The filaree (Erodium cicutarium) has become wonderfully successful as a world-traveler and colonizer in consequence of its cleverly constructed fruits. They are well adapted to steal free rides in the wool of sheep and on the tails of horses and cattle, but their native skill is best shown at planting time. Instead of being shot from their tiny cradles, each seed remains fastened to a long slender awn which twists into a spiral as it dries and untwists as it absorbs moisture. As a result of this corkscrew movement, the seed is forced into the ground, and germination is much more certain. In this way the filaree becomes established in places where other plants are unable to gain a foothold, and so it spreads at a tremendous rate. At times the little spirals cover the ground by the million and may be seen twisting and untwisting and pushing into the earth. In some parts of England they are fancifully imagined to be the needles used by the fairy Puck and are called Pook-needles.

YELLOW OXALIS

Oxalis corniculata

(Plate 5, fig. 5)

The yellow oxalis dots lawns and gardens, or borders roadsides with masses of clover-like leaves and bright flowers. It blooms all summer long and is widely distributed around the world as a number of named varieties, of which the common wood-sorrel (Oxalis stricta) of the East is one of the best known. In dry locations the plants are greatly dwarfed, sometimes growing but an inch or two tall with tiny blossoms, while in the shade they may stretch up to three feet high with flowers half an inch across. Occasionally the foliage changes color and forms bronze mats on lawns, or runs dark seams in the cracks of limestone copings.

The leaves have a pleasantly sour taste due to the oxalic acid they contain; they also possess the interesting habit of folding their leaflets together at sundown and quietly going to sleep. The flowers, too, may be considered "sleepy-heads," for they open only in late morning when the sun is warm enough to rouse them, and the petals fold together again in the early afternoon, long before the sun goes down. They do not open at all in bad weather or on cloudy days.

As the capsules mature, they stand erect like little candles and when ripe the merest touch will cause them to split apart and throw the seeds suddenly out in all directions. Under a magnifying glass each seed is seen to be bright orange-red in color, and shaped like a miniature top.

PINK OXALIS

OXALIS OREGONA

(Plate 5, fig. 6)

Loving moist shade, the pink oxalis carpets the redwood forest with attractive three-parted leaves that are so abundant as to almost conceal the scattered pale-pink blossoms, which are much larger than those of the yellow oxalis. This species ranges as far north as Washington, but is most characteristic of redwood groves along the coast. Cold damp woods of Canada, our own East, Europe and Asia are the haunts of a very near relative, the common wood-sorrel (Oxalis acetosella), which has white flowers with rosy veins. It is the leaves of this oxalis that are sometimes considered to be the original Irish shamrock.

The name oxalis is derived from a Greek word meaning sour, and this quality has given rise to the common name of sorrel, which is a diminutive of sour. Every child has eaten the leaves of the wood-sorrel, and even adults relish them in salads, sandwiches and pies. Some species furnish tuberous roots that are edible. Oxalic acid was first discovered in the plant, but is now prepared commercially by chemical processes and used in bleaching flax and straw, in the printing of calicoes and the removal of ink-stains. In its pure form this acid is very poisonous, but in plants it occurs as a salt of calcium which is not harmful though probably not desirable in a diet.

FLAX FAMILY

LINACEÆ

The flaxes are nearest the geraniums, with the pinks next in line. Their resemblance to oxalis is the closest, the distinguishing marks being the loss of five of the ten stamens and the simple narrow leaves on tall stems instead of three-parted leaves. The fruit is a round capsule and not elongated or beaked.

There are but a few principal genera in this family and among these there are very decided preferences for different climatic regions. One is European and Asiatic; another inhabits tropical Asia and still another the temperate parts of the Himalayas. The cultivated flax is one of the most useful of plants and is extensively grown, while some species from Europe and Africa with red, yellow, blue or white flowers are valued as ornamentals.

BLUE FLAX

LINUM PERENNE

(Plate 5, fig. 7)

A field of heavenly-blue flax is an enchanting sight early in the morning as the fragile blossoms on slender stems bend before the breeze. The petals fall before noon and the tiny-leaved plants then become inconspicuous until the new flowers bloom the next morning. Whether one travels from the coast to the Rocky Mountains, from the Arctic Circle to Mexico, or through Europe and Northern Asia, the blue flax nods a welcome from many a grassy field or shrubby hillside.

Despite their fleeting nature the flowers deserve a nook in the garden, though the scarlet flax (Linum grandiflorum) is more popular because of its gorgeous coloring and longer period of bloom. There are lovely yellow-flowered flaxes also; one (Linum berlandieri), is a native of Texas and Kansas, and smaller-flowered species grow in the East (Linum sulcatum) and Middle West (Linum rigidum). On languorous mornings in June they strew the prairies far and wide with fallen petals.

The name Linum is from a Greek word meaning thread, in

allusion to the use made of the unusually long and strong fibers found in the stems. The Indians of the Northwest utilize the fiber of the wild blue flax for making string or cord out of which they weave their mats, baskets, fish-nets, snow-shoes and all sorts of things. Longer and stronger fibers are secured from the flax native to southeastern Europe and Asia Minor (Linum usitatissimum), which has been cultivated from prehistoric times in the Old World and is now very much at home in the New World. Thousands of years ago linen threads were woven into cloth and today they are used in the finest lace and paper, as well as in coarse and heavy fabrics such as canvas, carpets and oilcloth, and in the strongest twine. It is but comparatively recently that the spinning-wheel to be found in every household has been replaced by modern machinery in the factory. Cotton produces its fibers in the seed-coats but the flax forms them in the stem and packs its seeds with an oil that has been found useful in many ways. It is employed by painters as linseed oil, while the residue left after its extraction from the seed is pressed into linseed cake and fed to cattle as an emergency ration. Flax seeds have a soothing effect on the mucous membranes, but have been known to cause unpleasant effects upon susceptible individuals who have eaten them in breakfast cereals.

The flax has always been associated in myths and legends with the idea of industry, and in certain districts of Germany brides were accustomed to place flax fiber in their shoes in the belief that it would protect them against future want.

ROCK-ROSE FAMILY

Cistaceæ

The rock-rose family is a small one with most of its members inhabiting the Mediterranean region, some in North America and a few elsewhere. The herbage is astringent and two or three species produce a fragrant resin that is used in perfumery. The methods of gathering this substance are unique and ingenious. Sometimes a flock of sheep is driven through the masses of plants and the resin sticks to their wool as they pass, or the foliage may be whipped with leather thongs which pick up the sticky droplets in a similar way.

The popular rock-roses of the garden belong to the type genus of the family (Cistus). They are low shrubs with many showy purple or white flowers, which resemble single roses superficially, but actually belong on the chart near the geraniums.

SUN-ROSE

Helianthemum scoparium

(Plate 6, fig. 1)

The fleeting blossoms of the sun-rose, starring low shrubby plants in the spring, are like the yellow flaxes to which they are closely related, and they also have the same habit of dropping their petals shortly after blooming. The plants, however, instead of being tall and slender with flexible stems like the flax, are somewhat woody, quite green and stiff, with small narrow leaves and a low bushy form which makes them suitable for garden borders.

The name helianthemum is from Greek words for sun and flower, in allusion to the fact that the blossoms open only in the sunshine. The many stamens resemble the cluster to be found in the roses and this has led to the name of sun-rose in spite of differences that determine actual relationships.

This California sun-rose is a hardy little pioneer in openings of the chaparral of the central and southern parts of the state and finds a foothold easily in burned-over areas. The frostweed (Helinthemum canadense), a near relative which may be found in the East, furnishes an interesting phenomenon on frosty autumn nights. In the crisp air, the sap which exudes from cracks in the roots freezes into glittering sheets of crystal.

ST. JOHNSWORT FAMILY

Hypericaceæ

The hypericums are natives of the temperate and hot portions of the globe, especially in the northern hemisphere. They all possess resinous juices, a volatile oil and a bitter extractive, which

Plate 6

ROCK-ROSE FAMILY

ST. JOHNSWORT FAMILY

PINK FAMILY

PURSLANE FAMILY

FOUR O'CLOCK FAMILY

BUCKWHEAT FAMILY

3
8
1
2
5
4
6
7

formerly gave them considerable use in medicine. The flowers of the family resemble roses superficially, but actually they are more like the rock-roses and they occupy a position on the family-tree near these.

ST. JOHNSWORT

HYPERICUM PERFORATUM

(Plate 6, fig. 2)

Though the St. Johnswort may outline roadsides with beautiful yellow bands or clothe fallow fields and pastures with gold, it is not at all attractive to the farmer. He finds it not only poisonous to his stock, but a troublesome weed very difficult to eradicate. It is a great traveler, having come to America from Europe, probably as a stowaway, and has been carried all over this country in the company of cereals and grains. It is very much at home in northern California and Oregon, where it blooms throughout the summer.

One of the most ornamental species in cultivation, known as Aarons-beard or rose-of-Sharon (Hypericum calycinum), has beautiful yellow flowers three inches in diameter, with a feathery group of stamens in the center. The wild St. Johnswort (Hypericum formosum), which prefers to dwell at moderate altitudes in weedy meadows and along streams, bears bright-yellow blossoms nearly an inch across that are much sought by bees for the abundant pollen. Higher up in the mountains and climbing to nearly 9,000 feet, the tinkers-penny (Hypericum anagalloides) covers moist soil with dense leafy mats, bright with dainty yellow blossoms.

The common name is due to the fact that the first flowers appear about June twenty-fourth, which is the day consecrated to St. John the Baptist. The reddish sap of the plants is also regarded as a symbol of this saint. Since St. John's day occurs in midsummer when the course of the sun covers the longest period, it was celebrated with ceremonies connected with sun-worship, and the bright-yellow flowers with sun-shaped disks took a prominent part in the rites and were consequently considered sacred to the saint. The symbolism is further carried out in the use of the plants as a sort of "scare-devil" to frighten away spirits of evil just as the sun's rays dissipate the darkness. For this purpose it was either burned, hung up over the door, or carried by the person wishing to be protected against harm.

The belief in the magical power of the St. Johnswort is of long standing, for the Greek name hypericum is derived from a verb meaning "to hold over in such a way as to protect from anything." The plants were used very long ago to heal all sorts of infirmities and even in later times were reputed in Brazil as an antidote for snake-bite, in Russia for hydrophobia and in England for insanity!

PINK FAMILY

Dianthaceæ

The pink family is also an offshoot from the geranium center, but in the direct line of advance toward the wind-pollinated buckwheats and goosefoots. They retain the ten stamens of their direct ancestors and the same number of petals and sepals, but the latter have united in some and the ovary shows an advance by a tendency to lose the cross-walls and reduce the number of chambers, frequently to one.

Representatives of the pink family show a preference for cooler climes, and are found as far north as the Arctic and on the summits of the highest Alps. There are but few medicinal plants in the number, but these range from such as furnish bitter astringents to those that yield syrups from sweet-scented petals. The inconspicuous little chickweed supplies many a caged bird with its daily rations of seeds while the gaily colored fragrant carnation represents the other extreme as a beautiful ornamental. Running a close second as favorites in the garden are babys-breath, catchfly, bouncing-bet, and ragged robin. With the notable exception of the Indian pinks, the wild-flower members of the group in this country have insignificant blossoms like those of the chickweeds, stichworts and pearlworts.

INDIAN PINK

Silene laciniata

(Plate 6, fig. 3)

Here and there in the shade of the chaparral or the tangled growth of canyons, the brilliant-red blossoms of the Indian pink contrast vividly with the dark background. Like many shade-loving plants, the stems are often tall and slender and bear the flowers loosely clustered. Both stems and leaves are covered with glandular hairs and feel sticky to the touch. Small insects such as gnats and mosquitoes find this stickiness too much for their delicate structure, and wings and feet become so entangled as to hold them prisoners for life. It is not at all likely that the plant makes use of their remains as insect-devouring plants do, the viscid excretion being merely a by-product, although it probably serves to render the herbage unpalatable to grazing animals. This characteristic is so marked in nearly related species as to win them the name of catchfly. The sleepy catchfly (Silene antirrhina) of the Yosemite and the East stays awake for but a short time in the sunshine, while the night-flowering catchfly (Silene noctiflora) wakes up at dusk and spends the entire night luring night-flying moths with its fragrant whiteness.

The narrow bases of the petals of the Indian pink are sheathed in the goblet-like calyx and the broader parts are turned back sharply at its edge, thus forming an excellent landing-platform for visiting insects. Sometimes the flowers hang rather obliquely from their stems and the lower petal is then seen to be especially modified to furnish a foothold for the bee in search of nectar. The ten anthers are grouped opposite this odd petal, five longer ones shedding their pollen first and five shorter ones later. While this is happening, the styles are closed together and hidden in the tube. The stigmas become receptive after the pollen is all shed and the anthers have curved back out of the way. As the flower wilts the petals shrink together, bringing anthers and stigmas into close contact. There is often enough pollen remaining to produce self-pollination as a last resort when cross-pollination has failed.

The Indian pink is common in southern and Lower California, where it blooms in late spring and summer, and it has traveled also as far eastward as New Mexico. In central and northern California and southwestern Oregon, it is replaced by a twin sister (Silene californica), which may be distinguished by the rounder lobes of the petals and oblong appendages on the corolla. The plants are usually taller also and the flowers often a deeper red.

Since Silenus, a companion of Bacchus in Greek mythology, has often been described as "covered with foam," the name Silene may have been given to the plant because of a soapy substance found in the roots which produces a suds when rubbed up with water. It seems more probable, however, that it is connected with the Greek word for saliva in allusion to the viscid excretion of the stalks. It might be assumed that the common name refers to the color of the flower, but in reality it goes back to an old-fashioned instrument called a pinking-iron. This was used to cut the edge of cloth or paper into a fringe such as characterizes not only the Indian pink but many carnations and other members of the family. Later this word came to designate the color as well as the flower.

PURSLANE FAMILY

Portulacaceæ

Although the purslane family is rather a small one, some species are present in every climate, but the majority favor the subtropical portions of the southern hemisphere. They furnish their contributions in the form of drugs, pot-herbs and ornamental plants. The best known and most beautiful of the last is the rose-moss, which is commonly called moss-rose. This covers the ground with a thick mat of trailing stems and fleshy leaves, ablaze with splendid flowers of many colors that are in great contrast to the delicate charm of the spring-beauties, their cousins in the East. A sort of poor relation to these richly clothed beauties is the common field purslane, with tiny yellow blossoms and flat succulent leaves. It is one of the globe-trotters among plants and has found its way along roadsides, into yards and fields everywhere, persisting by virtue of its creeping habit and multitude of seeds. In the Old

World it is often utilized as greens, though such a use is rare in this country. The miners-lettuce of the Pacific Coast was early used by the Indians as a salad or pot-herb, and is sometimes cultivated in England as well as America for the same purpose. Having specialized in succulent foliage, the flowers have been neglected and are small and white.

Another interesting species that grows in the West and Northwest is the bitter-root, with lovely pink or white many-petaled blossoms, sometimes two inches across, which open in the sunshine and close at evening. The Indians have found the large root to be quite edible if cooked, but exceedingly bitter when raw. These plants have the reputation of being able to stand drouth remarkably well and it is said that specimens laid away in the herbarium for a year or two have revived and bloomed again when planted.

Red-maids and spring-beauties suggest the relationship of the purslane family to the pinks, but they have departed from the ancestral habit by making the leaves fleshy, reducing the petals and producing ephemeral flowers. The thick leaves resist drouth successfully and the resulting conservation of their water supply may serve to explain the frequent great increase in the number of stamens. This occurs likewise in the cacti, and constitutes an interesting exception to the rule that numbers decrease with advancing specialization.

RED-MAIDS

Calandrinia caulescens

(Plate 6, fig. 4)

One must be on the alert to get a view of the brilliant rose-purple flowers of red-maids, for, besides being rather small and but one or two on each leafy stem, they open only in the sunshine. Moreover, they remain open but a few hours before wilting and deliquescing, and if gathered will close within a few minutes and steadfastly refuse to open again. The herbage of these plants furnished greens to the California Indians, who were also accustomed to roast the seeds for use in their bill-of-fare.

Red-maids are to be looked for in meadows and grassy openings along the Pacific Coast, from British Columbia to South America. The stems grow quite tall when overtopped by the grasses but are more or less recumbent on the open ground. The cultivated species (Calandrinia umbellata) has larger flowers of the same gorgeous color and is most effective when planted in sunny rockeries or borders.

FOUR O'CLOCK FAMILY

Nyctaginaceæ

The four o'clock family comprises herbs, shrubs and trees, which are widely distributed in warm climates but are most abundant in America. Their roots are purgative and emetic and are used for various disorders. A few of the four o'clocks are grown for ornament and of these the marvel-of-Peru and the bougainvilleas are the most popular and best known. The latter is a favorite porch-climber in California and southern climates generally, where it often makes gorgeous masses of color, by reason of the large purple or magenta bracts which enclose the inconspicuous flowers.

Many other four o'clocks also possess a brightly colored involucre that may be easily mistaken for the calyx and the bright calyx for the corolla. If their line of descent is traced, however, it seems probable that this group of plants long ago lost the corolla in response to wind-pollination and later changed the green calyx into a brightly colored one to replace the lost corolla. In turn, the tasks of the calyx were gradually assumed by the group of leaves below the blossoms and in some species these have come to completely simulate a calyx.

PINK ABRONIA

Abronia umbellata

(Plate 6, fig. 5)

Of the many gay flowers that carpet the strand with a cloth of many colors, none is more beautiful than the pink abronia. Its prostrate red or pink stems trail widely over the sand and send up thickish gray-green leaves and clusters of bright rose-purple flowers that are the most striking feature of the shore in summer and early autumn. Thriving best in the salt sea air, they overlook the rolling Pacific from British Columbia to Lower California.

From Santa Barbara south to San Diego, the dark red-purple flowers of the purple abronia (Abronia maritima) add their rich beauty to the scene and their fragrance to the air. It, too, has long trailing stems that take root at the joints and catch the sand as it is shifted about by the breeze, so that little sand-dunes are formed.

Both abronias receive attention from bees and butterflies that hover about the bright blossoms on sunny days and sip the nectar from the base of the slender flower-tubes. The fruits are four-angled and have thin papery wings that enable them to fly on the sea-breezes to new homes.

Although the abronias are commonly called sand-verbenas, the resemblance is merely a superficial one and the two flowers are only very distantly related. On the family-tree the mints and verbenas belong at the end of the line of insect-flowers sprung from the geranium, while the abronia is a four-o'clock and traces its lineage back to the pinks. The name abronia is both simple and pretty, and should be used to replace verbena. It is derived from the Greek for graceful or delicate and is well applied to these charming plants. In the garden they offer a change from the more commonplace verbena and will do well in sunny spots where the soil is light, especially in borders or in window-boxes and baskets.

The desert abronia (Abronia villosa) is a species of striking beauty that covers the Colorado and Gila deserts for miles during favorable winters with masses of fragrant pink bloom. It is smaller and more slender than the pink abronia of the coast, while the honey abronia (Abronia mellifera) of Washington and Oregon is stouter with large white blossoms. The fragrant abronia (Abronia fragrans), of eastern Washington and the prairies and plains of the Middle West, produces large clusters of sweet-smelling white flowers that open at night and close in the morning.

YELLOW ABRONIA

ABRONIA LATIFOLIA

(Plate 6, fig. 6)

The bright clusters of small blossoms, thick trailing stems and erect leaves of the yellow abronia ornament the sand-dunes of the coast, from Eureka northward to British Columbia. The flowers bloom in the spring and summer, filling the air with the delightful fragrance of heliotrope. Not only is this abronia attractive in appearance, but the long thick roots have been found useful additions to the food-supply of the Indians. In company with its pink and purple relatives, yellow abronias are especially well adapted to color massing in the wild garden where their preferences for a sandy soil should be respected.

WILD FOUR O'CLOCK

MIRABILIS CALIFORNICA

(Plate 6, fig. 7)

On cool afternoons from March to June, the pink or bright-magenta blossoms of the four o'clock add their beauty to the dry hillsides of southern California. By the next morning the slopes present quite a different appearance, for by this time the flowers have folded their gay banners and quietly gone to sleep. If the day is cool and cloudy, they remain open somewhat longer than when it is bright and dry, for, though pretty fancies may be woven about the movements of flowers, these are in reality controlled by temperature and moisture, which directly affect the flower mechanism. Four o'clock blossoms offer their honey to bees that work late in the afternoon or early in the morning, but especially to night-flying moths abroad at dusk.

The plants are low bushes with brittle, woody branches and sticky leaves that exhibit quite a range of color. This is consistent for any one individual, for the paler pink flowers are accompanied by green leaves and stems, while the glowing magenta ones grow on reddish stems with dark-green leaves and purplish involucres. There are often several buds enclosed by each involucre, but rarely is more than one at a time in bloom. In this way the nectar in each blossom is utilized to the maximum of efficiency.

The name mirabilis is taken from the Latin for wonderful or marvellous and was first applied to the large and gorgeously colored four o'clocks of the tropics, such as the marvel-of-Peru (Mirabilis jalapa) which has been cultivated since early times and is still a great favorite in old-fashioned gardens.

BUCKWHEAT FAMILY

POLYGONACEÆ

The buckwheats constitute a widespread family that has the greatest number of representatives in the northern hemisphere. Some of the genera that are large trees occupy tropical America and a few species find a retreat in the arctic zone, while the knot-weeds and docks are scattered everywhere from the seashore to the snow-line.

The mountains of Central Asia and North India are the original homes of the rhubarbs, which are prominent members of the family. In the tenth century they were spread through Europe by the Arabs, and several varieties are today widely cultivated for the sake of an important drug, as well as for the leaves and petioles, pleasantly acid in taste and hence esteemed for pies and preserves. The homely docks and sorrels also contain an acid of more or less value as a drug, but the knot-weeds have lost the repute they formerly enjoyed in medicine, except in China, Japan and Brazil, where some are still used. The cultivated buckwheat is one of the most prized plants because of the very fine honey it produces, as well as the most popular flour for griddle-cakes. This is obtained from the three-cornered seeds so like tiny beech-nuts that the name buckwheat is fashioned from an older form of the word beech.

Besides the wild buckwheat of California, Turkish rugging is the only wild-flower of this family which exhibits any particular beauty. This covers arid spots with a rough but rosy carpet in late spring, the entire plant being a harmony of crimson branches and pink blossoms. The pink hearts-ease of wet places is a common sight over most of the country, but princes-feather and the coral-vine are the only notable garden ornamentals.

WILD BUCKWHEAT

Eriogonum fasciculatum

(Plate 6, fig. 8)

Whether the wild buckwheat covers hillsides in spring with masses of feathery white bloom flushed with pink, or turns the dry slopes of midsummer to a rusty-red as the fruits ripen, it is often the dominant note of the chaparral of southern California. Since it requires little water and grows readily in rocky or gravelly places, it should be planted in similar situations in home gardens. That the wild buckwheat is able to survive in localities unfavorable to less hardy species, is shown by the fact that in a somewhat dwarfed form (Eriogonum polifolium) it invades the Mojave Desert and clings to the mountain slopes of Death Valley and Nevada as part of the desert scrub.

HEATH FAMILY

Ericaceæ

While America boasts some of the loveliest rhododendrons and azaleas and the fragrant trailing-arbutus, it lacks the true heathers that cover vast moorlands of England, Scotland and northern Europe with a rosy carpet. Their blossoms yield a honey with a sparkling color and unusual fragrance and flavor, which is of exceptional value in the market. The deservedly popular heaths in this country are the huckleberry, blueberry and cranberry, prized delicacies in the bill-of-fare, while oils, narcotics, astringents and acids are furnished by still other members of the family.

The heath family is here considered to comprise the closely allied pirolas and Indian-pipes, although these are often classed as separate families. The latter constitute a unique group of strangely colored plants that are parasitic on the roots of trees, especially pines and beeches. They belong to the leisure class in plant society that found a way of being supported by the workers in the plant world. Their ancestors were normal green plants able to manufacture their own food, but as they gradually learned to secure this from their neighbors they lost their chlorophyll and now appear in garbs of white, buff, yellow or crimson. Many species are sweet-scented like violets and pinks, but only one or two are of any use to man and even that is very local and limited in scope.

The pirolas are for the most part dainty wild-flowers that favor the cool or temperate mountain regions of the northern hemisphere, but one or two species have some useful medicinal properties.

BOG KALMIA

Kalmia polifolia

(Plate 7, fig. 1)

Where cold mountain streams rush noisily to add their waters to placid alpine lakes; where June snow-banks still linger in the shade of pine and spruce and high peaks tower dizzily, there is the favored haunt of the bog kalmia. One must step warily when in search of the rosy clusters of bowl-shaped blossoms, for the soil is boggy and the foot may slip from lake-shore or brook-bank into the water itself. A near view of these lovely flowers reveals them to be curiously pouched or angled, and in each of the tiny pockets there is held fast an anther so tautly that the filaments curve like little springs. Touch one of these ever so lightly and up it flies, pulling the anther free and shaking pollen out through a tiny hole in its end. By means of this ingenious mechanism, the bee is generously powdered as he probes busily for nectar, unaware that he is receiving a free dust-bath of pollen.

The woody stems of the bog kalmia, thickly set with leathery, glossy leaves, do not look especially succulent, but sheep are among the least particular of grazing animals and devour whatever is in their path. Many an innocent lamb and old sheep have paid for this lack of discrimination with their lives, for the kalmias are among the most poisonous of plants, as indicated by the common names of sheepkill and lambkill. Unfortunately, not only does danger to stock lurk in these attractive plants, but children also

PLATE 7

HEATH FAMILY

1
2
3
4
5
6
7
8
9

have paid the penalty for mistaking the leaves of young plants for those of wintergreen or checkerberry which they are fond of chewing.

The bog kalmia is decidedly partial to coolness and moisture, finding itself at home in bogs of the North from Newfoundland and Hudson's Bay to Sitka, and entering the States along the ridges of the Rockies and Sierra Nevada, where mountain lakes and streams spread out into swampy areas. Two very near relatives that occur abundantly in the rocky woodlands of eastern North America are the lambkill (Kalmia angustifolia) and the mountain kalmia (Kalmia latifolia). All three are beautiful hardy evergreens with showy clusters of purple, pink or nearly white flowers. The first two make attractive borders for shrubberies while the mountain kalmia is unusually ornamental, scattered over the lawn or grown in masses.

In spite of the fact that the kalmias are members of the heath family, the name of laurel is often applied, thus confusing them with the true laurel (Laurus) famed in legend and history as forming garlands for successful poet and victorious athlete. The latter belongs to the laurel family in the buttercup order and is far removed from the heaths.

YELLOW HEATHER

PHYLLODOCE GLANDULIFLORA

(Plate 7, fig. 2)

The tiny yellow heather forms small evergreen patches on rocks and cliff-edges in the mountains and hangs its clusters of sulphur-colored bells at the tips of short leafy stems. It is an inconspicuous little dwarf with a quaint charm suggestive of the elves and pixies with whom the heather is traditionally associated.

Nearly related to the red and yellow heathers is the white heather (Cassiope mertensiana), which may be found in the highest mountains as low-growing, thick patches of dark-green. The stems are woody and covered with small ridged leaves that overlap like fish-scales. The waxy white bell-shaped blossoms resemble lilies-of-the-valley in their trim beauty, in spite of their very different relationships.

The Greek name Phyllodoce is that of a sea-nymph mentioned by Virgil and fancifully applied to the exquisite blossoms of both the red and yellow heathers.

RED HEATHER

PHYLLODOCE EMPETRIFORMIS

(Plate 7, fig. 3)

Small patches of red heather are America's substitute for the vast stretches of the true heathers of Europe which belong to different nearly related genera (Calluna and Erica). Nevertheless, ours are just as charming as their foreign cousins, the nodding rose-purple blossoms growing in close clusters in company with the yellow and white heathers on the northern mountains. Another red heather (Phyllodoce breweri), with larger saucer-shaped flowers that are sweet-scented, seeks the high Sierra of California, and may be further distinguished by the protruding stamens and the deeply cleft corolla lobes.

BLUEBERRY

VACCINIUM CÆSPITOSUM

(Plate 7, fig. 4)

Clinging closely to Mother Earth, the stems of the blueberry, closely set with bright green leaves, must be lifted if the little pink globes of spring flowers or the dusky berries of late summer are to be seen. The plants rarely grow over six inches tall but sometimes cover the ground thickly in lodgepole forests or even higher up in the mountains, above the line where timber can grow at all. Though the berries of this species are fairly large and sweet, those of the Sierra blueberry (Vaccinium occidentale) are bigger and better. The plants grow in similar localities, but may reach two feet in height with berries a quarter of an inch across and almost black.

For some reason, the name Vaccinium is connected with the Latin word for cow, while the common name of bilberry, sometimes used, is corrupted from bull-berry. There is great confusion in the application of the names blueberry, huckleberry and cranberry, with a tendency, perhaps, to restrict the use of the first to the species with berries of a lighter hue and sometimes with a "bloom." The dark purple or shiny black berries are called huckleberries and the red ones cranberries. The true cranberry, however, is often placed in a different genus (Oxycoccus).

CALIFORNIA HUCKLEBERRY

Vaccinium ovatum

(Plate 7, fig. 5)

The California huckleberry is compelling in its beauty at all seasons, whether bedecked with clusters of dainty pink blossoms in spring and summer, hung with purplish-black berries later in the season, or merely clothed in shining evergreen leaves. Its manifold attractions are in a fair way, however, to bring about its complete disappearance from the coastal hills of California and redwood openings in western Oregon, for at Christmas-time the branches are brought into the cities by the ton for household decoration. Scarcely less eagerly is it sought for the sake of the edible berries which make excellent preserves and which furnish another reason for protecting the plants themselves.

The highbush blueberry (Vaccinium corymbosum) of northeastern North America, is also an exceedingly ornamental shrub and well-adapted to many a setting. Not only are the blossoms attractive and the fruit of the best, but the foliage turns brilliantly crimson or scarlet in the autumn. Since the plants are eight or ten feet tall and spreading, the effect is unsurpassed. The flowers furnish excellent honey and in some parts of New England beekeepers depend upon them for their supply in May and June. The honey-bees are forced to pass by the stamens on their way to the concealed nectar and in so doing brush against ingenious little appendages, that cause the pollen to be shaken out of tiny holes in the ends of the anthers.

MANZANITA

ARCTOSTAPHYLUS TOMENTOSA

(Plate 7, fig. 6)

Of the many shrubs found in the chaparral of coastal hills, none is more characteristic or better known than the manzanita. Its claim to distinction lies, not only in the beauty of the pale foliage and clusters of pink, vase-like blossoms combined with red-brown branches, but also in the usefulness of flowers, wood and berries. The blossoms yield an excellent brand of honey of fine flavor and light amber color. The branches are hard and polished, shedding their thin, shreddy, cinnamon-colored bark every season, but they are too crooked to be made into anything more practical than walking-sticks. The unripe berries are utilized for jelly and subacid beverages, but on maturity they become dry and mealy and are then eaten by the Indians, either raw or cooked. When indulged in too freely, they produce undesirable results and had best be left for the bears. These animals are so fond of the rosy fruits that this species and some other nearly related ones are called bear-berry. The scientific name arctostaphylus is formed from Greek words for bear and grape, and is said to refer to the furry coat of the young berries, while the Spanish name of manzanita means little apple and alludes to the redness of the fruits.

Another bear-berry (Arctostaphylus uva-ursi) is widespread in almost all northern countries around the world, but in many localities it is also called by the Indian name of kinnikinnic. In the East it prefers sandy pine-barrens and in the Middle West the sandy shores of lakes where it forms dunelets. In the Rocky Mountains and the coast ranges of Oregon, it covers stony, disintegrated soil with thick evergreen mats of shining leaves mingled with waxen, white flowers in early spring and crimson berries through the summer and fall. Birds, as well as bears and other animals, are fond of the fruit and it is quite likely that the wide distribution of the species is due to their having carried the seeds in distant flights. The leaves are smoked by the Indians and are used in medicine for their astringent qualities, as well as in tanning the finer kinds of leather and in dyeing gray or black.

SALAL

GAULTHERIA SHALLON

(Plate 7, fig. 7)

Forming a fretted evergreen layer in redwood or fir forests as far north as Washington, the salal puts forth slender flowering stalks in the spring and early summer and hangs each with a row of drooping bells. As the season advances and the bees perform their appointed tasks, the blossoms give way to purple-black berries which look like small grapes and have a spicy flavor. Ever on the lookout for something new to tickle or satisfy the appetite, the Oregon Indians have long made use of these in syrups or to add flavor to soups of boiled roots.

Although the salal may boast of but few near relatives, the wintergreen (Gaultheria procumbens) of eastern and northern evergreen woodlands, is well-known for its contribution of oil-of-wintergreen. This fragrant oil was first found in these pretty little creeping plants, with their waxen, white flowers and scarlet berries, but it is now more easily obtained by chemical methods than by distillation from the leaves. It has many and varied uses: from that of a liniment to flavoring for chewing-gum; from a medicine to a scent for soap. Like many another medicine, it becomes poisonous in overdoses. Since children are in the habit of chewing the spicy leaves and berries of wintergreen, they should be taught to distinguish them clearly from the young seedlings of kalmia that are similar in appearance but extremely poisonous.

WESTERN AZALEA

RHODODENDRON OCCIDENTALE

(Plate 7, fig. 8)

Difficult as it may be to award a prize for beauty to any one species, the azaleas and rhododendrons form a group of shrubs unexcelled for their showy flowers and charming foliage. Though the latter are usually evergreen and the former deciduous, they are scarcely otherwise to be distinguished, each competing with the other in brilliance or delicacy of coloring and profusion of bloom. For charm the western azalea ranks among the foremost, the fragrant, white blossoms, faintly flushed with rose-color and ornamented with yellow, turning the margins of mountain streams into banks of beauty from early June to the end of July. Unforgettable memories of their loveliness are the rewards of visitors to the Yosemite or other resorts in the Sierra Nevada and Coast Ranges.

The name rhododendron is formed from Greek words meaning rose-tree but since the flowers are not roses and the plants are shrubs of ten feet or less in height, the word is scarcely descriptive of this genus. It is possible that the first-named azalea was found in a dry or arid spot, for that is the meaning of this word, but the western azalea is a moisture-loving plant.

For shrubbery in a cool climate, no mistake will be made in choosing any of the rhododendrons or azaleas for grouping or growing singly here and there. There are about three hundred and fifty native species to be found in the cool and temperate regions of the northern hemisphere and a large number of garden hybrids so that the range of choice is unusually wide. Some are useful as well as ornamental, the close-grained wood being suitable for fuel or the construction of various turned articles. Drugs are obtained from the leaves, and the fruits of some East Indian species furnish a subacid jelly. Cases of poisoning have been reported from the use of the honey, but this danger may be recognized by the pungent taste and peculiar smell, or avoided by permitting the honey to become well ripened beforehand. It is said that the honey which maddened Xenophon's soldiers during the retreat of the Ten Thousand was collected from a species of either azalea or rhododendron, both of which abound on the shores of the Euxine.

SNOW-PLANT

Sarcodes sanguinea

(Plate 7, fig. 9)

The vivid red shafts of the snow-plant, thickly clustered with hanging bell-shaped flowers of glowing hue, shoot up like magic through the carpets of needles which have been spread by the yellow pine during the winter. They are among the very earliest of spring flowers to take advantage of the abundant moisture left by melting snow-banks. The plants are so striking by reason of their fiery translucence that they were in a fair way to become exterminated until protected by man-made regulations, and even at their best today they occur only as scattered individuals and small colonies here and there in the Sierras.

The names used for the genus and species are from Greek and Latin terms for flesh-like and blood, the former applying to the character of both stalk and flowers and the latter to their color. The name snow-plant reflects the popular belief in the location of the plants in the midst of snow-banks, but in reality they grow at the edges of these or in wet places left by the melted snow.

The snow-plant is the most brilliantly garbed of this whole group of parasites, the Indian-pipe (Monotropa uniflora) being a creamy white and forming small ghost-like groups in dark damp woods, while the pine-sap (Hypopitys americana) is a pale lemon-yellow. The former is rare in California, but the latter is widespread in the forests of Oregon, British Columbia and throughout the northern hemisphere.

PINK PIROLA

Pirola rotundifolia

(Plate 8, fig. 1)

Spicy spruce woods, running mountain brooks and invigorating air mark the spots where the pink pirola sends up single flower stalks hung with pendant coral blossoms. These are faintly fragrant and the waxen petals, pale-pink or tinged with shades deepening to carmine, cluster prettily about the pistil with its down-curving style. The leaves are as characteristic as the oddly shaped flowers and form a rosette at the base of the stem. They are quite round, with long stalks and scalloped edges, thick, leathery and a shining dark-green.

The pink pirolas grow in boreal and mountain habitats in Europe and Asia as well as in this country. Although not as abundant in California as the leafless pirola (Pirola aphylla) and the

Plate 8

HEATH FAMILY

PRIMROSE FAMILY

LEADWORT FAMILY

1
2
3
4
5
6

shin-leaf (Pirola picta), they occur on Mount Rainier, around Lake Tahoe and in the Yosemite. Other species in England are also called shin-leaf by the country-folk who use the leaves in plasters for bruises and sores.

Since the flowers of the pink pirola possess but little fragrance and no nectar, they attract few insects. They have, however, perfected an ingenious method of self-pollination. The anthers sift the pollen out through tiny pores when the stigma is curved back out of the way at first. Later it turns forward in line with them to catch the falling pollen.

PALE PIROLA

PIROLA MINOR

(Plate 8, fig. 2)

The creamy balls of the pale pirola, flushed with pink, resemble half-opened buds even when in full bloom. They may be distinguished from the pink pirola by the paler tints and short straight style hidden within the petals. The green pirola (Pirola secunda) also has a straight style, but the flowers are greenish and attached to the stalk in a lop-sided fashion. Another species (Pirola chlorantha) hangs its greenish-white blossoms on the stalk in the usual way, but these have curved styles like those of the pink pirola.

The pale pirola is scarce in the Sierra Nevada though present in the Yosemite, but it is quite abundant in Oregon and farther north. All these pirolas are lovers of cool northern and mountain woods throughout most of North America, Europe and Asia and may be grown in moist, shady nooks in the garden. Of near relatives, the pipsissewa (Chimaphila umbellata) is very like the pirolas in some ways, but differs in the waxen, creamy flowers clustered on leafless stems, while the single-beauty (Moneses uniflora) is a charming little dwarf with but one flower. This is a sweetly fragrant blossom, about three-quarters of an inch across, that hangs pendant at the tip of a leafless stem, rarely more than four inches tall.

The flowers of the pale pirola are nectarless, but the stigma possesses a sticky substance which attracts numbers of beetles. These visitors are in the habit of licking this exudation and, in so doing, leave some pollen brought from other flowers.

PRIMROSE FAMILY

Primulaceæ

The primrose family takes its name from the most important genus Primula, which means the "first flower of spring." The English "primrose" is a corruption of an old French word "primerole" and has nothing to do with the rose. The plants grouped under this family name are regarded as descendants of the pinks, their most significant advance being the union of the petals into a tube and the reduction of the stamens from ten to a single row of five.

Most of the species are from the temperate regions of Europe and Asia and many of them seek the high altitudes of the mountains. They are valued more highly as ornamentals than as sources of useful products and comprise some lovely wild-flowers as well as popular greenhouse and garden plants. The cyclamen of the florist is a favorite house-plant and when properly cared for will produce an abundance of white or purple blossoms and attractive leaves over a long period of time. The European species of cyclamen has very fragrant bright-red flowers which win it the name of bleeding-nun. Cyclamen flowers are very like those of our wild shooting-star in form, but are much larger.

Many species of the primrose proper are grown in borders and rockeries and several are among the most popular greenhouse and florists' plants. Other members of the family that are garden favorites are the rose-colored rock-jasmines, yellow loosestrifes and the large flowered pimpernels.

SCARLET PIMPERNEL

Anagallis arvensis

(Plate 8, fig. 3)

In mid-morning of clear days, the coral-red blossoms of the scarlet pimpernel glow on their spreading mats of bright leaves like jewels against green silk. Although rarely more than two flowers on a leafy stem are open at the same time, the plants cover considerable areas and the mass of bloom forms one of the distinctive features of fallow field or garden not too well tended. It is a cheery little weed that has come over from the Old World and is content with waste places everywhere, though preferring the coast to the warm interior.

The small flat blossoms are borne on slender stalks in the axils of the leaves and bloom successively from the lower part of the stem towards the tip. So it may be, as the buds unfold, that the flowers just below them have dropped their petals and those still further away have formed fruits that hang downward on curving stalks. As a result, pollinating insects are attracted over the longest period of time with the least waste of energy and material. In case insect visitors are lacking, self-pollination is resorted to. When a blossom opens about nine o'clock in the morning of a sunny day, the stigma is all ready to receive pollen brought from other flowers. The anthers crack two or three hours later, and when the flower closes at about three o'clock in the afternoon the three lowermost ones are forced into contact with the stigma and deposit pollen on its sticky surface. Since the flowers open and close three days in succession, there is little chance of any remaining unfertilized. Such tiny blossoms are able to offer but limited landing-space for the larger pollinating insects, but small bees and butterflies, such as "skippers" and "blues," are welcomed.

The Greek name anagallis is from words meaning "to delight in again" and probably has reference to the flower's habit of reopening in bright sunshine. It has thus come about that the genus is reputed not only to possess the power of removing despondency but of preventing witchcraft. In England it is called Shepherd's-clock and Johnny-go-to-bed-at-noon, because of the early afternoon closing of the blossoms. Poor-man's-weather-glass is another name still used by country-folk in England who relied upon the sensitiveness of the petals to the humidity in the air as foretelling changes in weather. This was considered even more reliable than the barometer and whenever the flowers expanded fully in the morning no rain was to be expected that day, but if they failed to open at all, showers were looked for.

Pimpernels may be easily grown in warm soil. There are some varieties with large blue or white flowers and others with rose-colored or purplish ones. The seeds are formed in quaintly shaped little fruits called pixie-caps. These are small round boxes that split around the middle when ripe, the upper part resembling a tiny peaked cap and coming off like a lid.

SHOOTING-STAR

Dodecatheon meadia

(Plate 8, fig. 4)

The shooting-stars are the first to take advantage of winter rains or melted snows as they spread a rosy carpet over the hill-sides for the advancing feet of Spring. They range from the Atlantic to the Pacific, from Michigan to Texas, from Lower California to the Behring Straits; they are frequent in the Rocky Mountains and abundant in the Yosemite and Hetch Hetchy. How many species and varieties there may be in these various localities is a question of more interest to the specialist than to the nature lover, especially as there seems to be considerable disagreement on the subject.

The Greek name of the genus apparently has no significance, since it means twelve gods, although it has been suggested as indicating that the primrose is under the care of the deities. The name shooting-star, however, aptly describes the way in which the petals flare backwards, like the tail of a comet, from the sharp point formed by the stamens which are thrust forward from the corolla.

STAR-FLOWER

Trientalis europæa

(Plate 8, fig. 5)

The pale sunshine that filters down through the overarching canopy of redwood trees is taken full advantage of by the thin leaves of the star-flower as they spread out horizontally close to the sun-flecked ground. Poised above on thread-like stems are dainty blossoms like seven-pointed pink stars.

Contrary to the rule, the deep shade in which the plants are found does not cause them to stretch up to unusual heights. They rarely grow to more than the "third of a foot" tall, which is indicated by the name trientalis. Dimly lighted woods in Europe and Asia, as well as in the Coast Ranges from California to Alaska, shelter this star-flower or its varieties, while the damp forests of the East are the home of a white-flowered species (Trientalis americana).

Shade-loving plants are apt to be neglected by butterflies and bees, but, to any that may happen to wander into the shadows, the star-flower offers a drink of nectar which is stored in a fleshy ring at the base of the ovary. In the complete absence of chance visitors, the closing of the petals brings any pollen that may be clinging to the anthers at the time into close contact with the stigma and results in self-pollination.

LEADWORT FAMILY

Plumbaginaceæ

The leadworts are cosmopolitan in their tastes with a preference for saline situations. The family name is taken from that of an important genus and means lead, since there is a fatty substance in the root that imparts a leaden color to paper or fingers. This is very caustic and was formerly used in medical practice, but seems to be employed today only by beggars who wish to excite pity by their sores, using it in much the same way as the juice of some buttercups. One of the South African species of leadwort is popular in the greenhouse and gardens of warm climates on account of its lovely clusters of azure-blue blossoms. The sea-lavenders are also favorites in hothouses and rockeries and some are grown extensively along the coast for everlasting bouquets, since the bright-colored papery corollas keep their beauty when dried.

SEA-THRIFT

Armeria vulgaris

(Plate 8, fig. 6)

The sea-thrift on sandy beach or grassy cliff lifts cushion-like heads of tiny lavender flowers and overlooks the ocean, from California to Alaska and from Labrador to Quebec. It loves the salt air, and, thriving best in breezes from the sea, well deserves its name. The plants are easy to grow and the rosettes of narrow evergreen leaves at the base of the flower stalks are admirably adapted to borders in the garden and to edgings along the walks.

GENTIAN FAMILY

Gentianaceæ

It is said that over two thousand years ago the army of King Gentius of Illyria suffered from malarial fever and that this king succeeded in checking it by means of the bitter tonic in the plants which now bear his name. This drug consequently gained such repute as to be used as an antidote of the plague and the bites of mad dogs, as well as a remedy for many diseases, but today its main value is that of a simple bitter.

There are many lovely wild gentians in different parts of the world, but they show a special liking for haunts in the mountains and are especially abundant in the high Alps. As a consequence but few respond to cultivation, although there are several that might be induced to occupy suitable spots in the wild garden.

BLUE GENTIAN

Gentiana calycosa

(Plate 9, fig. 1)

The blue gentians make an entrance on the scene long after the gay procession of spring flowers have gone to seed and only late-summer laggards linger in sheltered places, and then they hold the center of the stage until Jack Frost rings down the curtain. More deeply blue than the sky, they raise deep chalices on leafy stems of smooth shining green, furnishing inspiration to the poet, "gentian-blue" to the artist's palette and nectar to bumble-bees that forage late in mountain meadows.

This blue gentian of the Sierra Nevada and Cascades is essentially the same as that of the Rocky Mountains. The sky-blue fringed gentian (Gentiana crinita) of the East is so eagerly sought by flower vandals as to be threatened with extinction in spite of its success in attracting bumble-bees and excluding harmful insects by means of the fringe. The fringed gentian of the Rockies (Gentiana serrata) is similar in shape, but is a dark purple-blue in color.

Both the blue and the fringed gentians have the habit of opening in the morning and closing in the afternoon, but the closed gentians (Gentiana affinis, G. andrewsi) open so slightly as to deserve their name. On cold mornings, the temperature of the air within the corolla may be several degrees warmer than that outside. Bumble-bees force their way into these closed chambers in their determination to secure the nectar even at the expenditure of much effort.

The striking difference in the habits of these two groups of gentians has been accounted for in a fanciful story. This relates that originally all gentians were closed, but that once upon a time the Queen of the Fairies had been kept so busy with tasks incident to All-Hallows' Eve that the moon went down and the fireflies to bed before she noticed that it was too dark to find her way home. As it was late in the season, there were no flowers about except those of the closed gentian. She hastened from one to another of these, asking it to please open up and give her shelter for the night. The blossoms were too sleepy to be kind and refused her requests crossly, one after the other. Finally, one seemed less selfish and agreed to let the Fairy Queen sleep within its closed chamber. As a reward the flower was granted the power to open each day and thus it has come about that the fringed gentians greet the sun in the morning and close at his setting.

Plate 9

GENTIAN FAMILY

DOGBANE FAMILY

MILKWEED FAMILY

1
2
3
4
5

ROSE GENTIAN

Gentiana amarella

(Plate 9, fig. 2)

The individual flowers of the rose gentian have an appealing charm in their daintiness and pale coloring, quite different from that of the dark beauty of the blue gentians. They are small, with pale creamy tubes and sharply turned-back pointed lobes of rose-lavender, and a pretty lavender fringe at the edge of the throat. They have traveled further afield than the larger gentians and may be greeted by the traveler in Arctic America, Europe and Asia, if he visit their favorite haunts in the mountains—whether the Rockies, Carpathians or those that cluster thickly about the great deserts of Tibet and Mongolia.

Having wandered far and wide over the face of the earth, like other world-travelers the plants of the rose gentian are adaptable and adjust themselves to changing conditions readily and completely. In the deep shade of spruce woods, they may become two feet tall and slender, stretching up toward the light, with broad thin leaves adapted to making the most of the weak illumination. Exposed to the full strength of the sun, the plants grow quite bunchy, with thicker leaves, and bear many flowers. Such as strike root in dry gravel-slides or alpine rock-fields are unable to secure enough food for full growth and so remain tiny dwarfs—in extreme cases half an inch tall with but one flower. All variations and gradations occur between these widely divergent forms in response to degree of shade or moisture available in meadows, open woodlands or above timber-line. The flowers range in color from white through pale-lavender to deep rose-purple, while the herbage may be dark-green or tinged with red.

Like most other gentians, the rose gentian opens in the morning and closes in the afternoon. The nectar is secreted at the base of the corolla-tube where bumble-bees search for it, thrusting the head into the mouth of the corolla until it touches the anthers and stigma, and then unrolling the proboscis to the bottom of the tube. The fine fringe on the petals curves over the opening of the flower-tube so that unwelcome guests are excluded.

ERYTHRÆA

ERYTHRÆA VENUSTA

(Plate 9, fig. 3)

Few flowers can compete in brilliancy of effect with the erythræa which covers the barer spots of dry hills and grassy mesas with masses of rose-purple bloom. This may be due in part to the contrast afforded by the background, though the color itself is so unusually pure and vivid as to be noted in the name, which means red. At their best, the plants grow a foot or more tall and quite branched, bearing such a profusion of blossoms that each becomes a complete bouquet. A persistent search in spots with especially hard or dry soil will reveal tiny specimens but an inch or so high, each with a single flower.

The erythræa is very much of a stay-at-home, rarely venturing beyond the limits of central and southern California, though it does not object to climbing the mountains into the Yosemite and Hetch Hetchy Valleys. Its favorite locations are in bare, sandy soil that is shaded somewhat by grasses or taller herbs and shrubs.

The need of these plants for comparatively little moisture and their appearance in summer after the spring flowers have finished blooming, is sufficient recommendation for their introduction into the wild garden, even if they were less showy in appearance.

Early settlers in California as well as native Indians, called this species canchalagua and valued it for its tonic properties, which are similar to those of other gentians.

DOGBANE FAMILY

APOCYNACEÆ

The dogbanes are very much at home in the warm countries of the world and especially so in Asia beyond the equator. Among them may be found many of the handsomest and most fragrant species and some of the most useful, as well as a number that are intensely poisonous. The original meaning of the name indicates that this poison may have been used against canine pests. The savages of the tropics still utilize it on their arrow-points, and in

Madagascar the ordeal-tree is employed as a test of innocence or guilt. The accused person is compelled to swallow the pounded kernel of a nut from this tree, one seed of which is sufficient to kill twenty people. The assumption is that if the suspected person is innocent the poison will be immediately rejected by the stomach, while if guilty it will be absorbed and death quickly follow.

The flowering shoots of the oleander are also actively poisonous, and bark and leaves are used in rat poisons. Death has resulted from using the wood as meat-skewers, and since the oleanders are frequently planted as ornamental shrubs, the danger should be recognized. Other members of the dogbane family furnish wood for carving and furniture, fiber-plants, some edible fruits and India rubber, while in the garden there are vines, shrubs and small trees as well as herbs. Of these, besides the sweet-scented and evergreen oleanders, the most popular are allamanda, plumeria, the Natal-plum and periwinkle.

DOGBANE

APOCYNUM ANDROSÆMIFOLIUM

(Plate 9, fig. 4)

The low shrubs of the dogbane, with loose clusters of dainty pink and white blossoms hidden among dark-green leaves, often form pretty borders to thickets in the East as well as the West. They are very abundant along the Missouri River in Kansas and Missouri, and in some places in British Columbia the plants cover hundreds of acres. They are especially valued in these regions as honey-producers. The flowers are so fragrant as to attract bees in large numbers, and the honey is excellent and practically colorless. The dogbane is also available when other honey-plants have disappeared, since it blooms over an unusually long period.

The flowers are ingeniously constructed to protect the nectar against extraction by any insect except those that bring about pollination. The red streaks on the pale petals guide the bee to the honey which is secreted at the base of the corolla and covered by hairs on the stamen filaments. The anthers are grown together in such a way as to form a sort of trap that catches smaller insects and prevents them from stealing the nectar. The larger bees are strong enough to draw the proboscis out after sucking the honey, although even for them considerable force is necessary to escape being held prisoners.

The milky juice of the dogbane, which blisters the skin and is somewhat used in medicine, has recently been found to yield as much as five per cent of good rubber. The Indian hemp (Apocynum cannabinum) is not only a promising native rubber plant but produces a useful drug and a stout fiber which is strong enough for twine, fish-nets, baskets, etc., and if treated properly emerges soft and white and suitable for weaving into cloth. This species is a taller plant than the dogbane and has small greenish-white flowers. It grows frequently in moist places, but is especially abundant in the lower parts of the Yosemite Valley.

MILKWEED FAMILY

Asclepiadaceæ

The milkweeds inhabit the same countries as the dogbanes and are to be found especially in tropical and subtropical regions. Both families possess a milky juice, and indeed are so much alike in many respects as formerly to have been classed together. It is this juice that makes some of the milkweeds rubber plants with commercial possibilities and in others is the source of arrow-poisons and many useful drugs. It is due to their value in this last respect that the most important genus was named after Asclepias, the god of medicine. Some East Indian species yield tenacious fibers and others dyes.

There are many beautiful wild species of milkweed in this country and a few are planted in borders, but as a rule they are neglected in favor of other garden plants.

SHOWY MILKWEED

Asclepias speciosa

(Plate 9, fig. 5)

Early in the season, the showy milkweed hangs heavy clusters of purple blossoms on plants that seem frosted over, so thick are the fine white hairs covering stem and leaf. Later, when asters and goldenrods claim the meadows and brown cat-tails in the marshes turn to fuzzy-yellow, the pods hang dimmed by a mist of silver silk as the tiny brown seeds forsake their satin-lined cradles to float lazily on the wind.

The peculiar shape of the milkweed blossom is intimately related to the visits of bees and butterflies. They are attracted by a sweet fragrance, but after sipping the nectar are held fast in a tiny trap until the concealed pollen-sacs become fastened to some part of their bodies. These twin sacs look very like a pair of diminutive saddle-bags, clipped together at their upper ends by a gummy substance which sticks so tenaciously that the clips frequently remain fastened to the insect after the sacs have been deposited on a receptive stigma. It is said that many a bee has lost its life in the end by becoming overburdened with the accumulation of clips or by failing to get free from the trap. Nevertheless, honey-bees find the attraction irresistible, and a single colony will often produce from fifty to one hundred pounds of excellent milkweed honey. The nectar is so eagerly sought by butterflies also that the orange-red milkweed (Asclepias tuberosa) of the East and Middle West is known as the butterfly-weed.

The whorled milkweed (Asclepias galioides) and the woolly-pod milkweed (Asclepias eriocarpa) sometimes poison sheep that are unusually hungry, since well-fed stock are not tempted by them. The silkweed (Asclepias syriaca) not only charms with a delightful fragrance but also produces tender shoots in the spring that are used as pot-herbs, as well as fine silky hairs on the seeds that the French Canadians stuff into mattresses, and so much nectar in the flower that these are collected in the morning when covered with dew and made into a sugar. The desert milkweed (Asclepias subulata) excels in the amount of caoutchouc in its juice, which makes it the best of our native rubber plants. It is leafless for most of the year, consisting of a cluster of rush-like stems often six to ten feet tall, and thrives in the Gila, Colorado and Mojave Deserts in an annual rainfall of one to three inches. The fiber has been found to be of excellent quality and can be made into fine writing paper.

Many of the milkweeds are perennials of the easiest cultivation. The large-leaved varieties are desirable for their masses of foliage, while the butterfly-weed with orange-red blossoms, showy milkweed with purplish ones and the swamp milkweed (Asclepias incarnata) with dark-crimson clusters offer a range of striking color during their period of blooming.

PHLOX FAMILY

POLEMONIACEÆ

This large and attractive family of flowering plants is almost entirely North American, with a few members residing in the temperate and cold regions of Europe and Asia. Practically all have specialized in beauty rather than utility, only one species yielding a drug of merely local use and the rest comprising many of our most attractive wild-flowers and garden ornamentals. Their number is greatest along the Pacific Coast, where many of the wild species are being introduced into home gardens. They take readily to cultivation and many of the gilias and polemoniums respond with a wealth of bloom. Phloxes, or sweet Williams, are among the showy occupants of the garden and are better known because of the longer time they have been under cultivation, while cobæas are climbers of less familiar aspect.

SCARLET GILIA

GILIA AGGREGATA

(Plate 10, fig. 1)

In midsummer, gravel-slides in the mountains are clothed in scarlet as the tiny trumpets of this gilia flare out from the stem and seem to call butterflies and humming-birds to a banquet of sweets. Bumble-bees know well that their short tongues cannot reach to the bottom of the long, slender tube and rarely even stop to look, but when the sun goes down and birds and butterflies have folded their wings for the night, moths appear on the scene and make the rounds as long as they can see the blossoms in the dusk.

The scarlet gilia is a showy biennial that seeks its favored haunts on high sagebrush plains in the Middle West and warm mountain slopes at six to ten thousand feet. The variety to be found in the Rocky Mountains differs from that of the Yosemite and Coast ranges in the shorter, blunter lobes of the corolla and in a wider range of color. It is usually a lovely pink at the higher altitudes, while the flowers that bloom on the plains at the foot of the mountains are more frequently white or scarlet.

GLOBE GILIA

Gilia capitata

(Plate 10, fig. 2)

The globe gilia is deservedly a favorite because of its dense, round clusters of lavender-blue blossoms and finely cut foliage. The plants spring up in abundance in open places and grasslands of the coast, from California to Washington, and bloom during the spring and early summer. They grow remarkably well in the garden, yielding a profusion of bloom and foliage in return for very little care.

Another blue gilia (Gilia c. achillæfolia) of the coast region is a variety that differs in a stouter habit, larger looser clusters of flowers and more feathery light-green leaves. It is abundant in the Yosemite where the globe gilia is found rather less frequently.

BIRDSEYE GILIA

Gilia tricolor

(Plate 10, fig. 3)

The birdseye gilia combines yellow in the tube of the flower with purplish-brown spots at the base of the lavender-blue petals in such a way as to resemble the vari-colored eyes of certain birds. The blossoms are comparatively large and prettily clustered on graceful stems with finely cut foliage. They grow wild on the hillsides of central California, from coast to mountain, but will thrive in the garden with little care, and bloom profusely. White, rose-colored or red-violet flowers are borne by cultural forms of the same species and complete a most charming range of color.

Plate 10

PHLOX FAMILY

1
2
3
4
5
6
7
8

BUFF GILIA

GILIA GRANDIFLORA

(Plate 10, fig. 4)

The buds of the buff gilia are a pale-yellow and the full-blown flowers a soft buff-color which turns a salmon-pink as they fade. The blossoms are borne in showy terminal clusters on leafy stems and have long tubes with recurved corolla-lobes. The plants thrive best in warm situations, taking readily to openings in the mountains and foothills up to 6,000 feet, and growing abundantly in the Yosemite and its vicinity. They are found also as far north as British Columbia and east to Idaho and Nevada.

PRICKLY GILIA

GILIA CALIFORNICA

(Plate 10, fig. 5)

Most beautiful of all the gilia group, the prickly gilia sharply resents being ruthlessly gathered and is so surrounded by spiny foliage that it does not require the protection of flower preservation societies. The rose-pink blossoms, with satin petals, cover low shrubs in the chaparral from Los Angeles to Monterey. They have a sweet fragrance and though not hardy in the East, are adapted to sunny spots, rock-nooks and low hedges in the gardens of mild climates. An annual pink gilia (Gilia densiflora) resembles the prickly gilia somewhat, but it lacks the spiny tips to the leaves and the flowers are a trifle smaller with veins of a darker pink than the petals, or they may even be pure-white. This blooms so profusely in the garden as to make unusually striking borders or low masses.

FEATHER GILIA

GILIA ANDROSACEA

(Plate 10, fig. 6)

The dainty little plants of the feather gilia bloom unobtrusively among the grasses and shrubs of the lower altitudes in the

Sierra and Coast Ranges. The long lavender-blue flowers on thread-like stalks form loose clusters within a whorl of narrow leaves. They are inconspicuous enough to pass unnoticed among their companions of spring—poppies, cream-cups and bærias—except when growing densely enough to form beds.

FRINGED GILIA

GILIA DIANTHOIDES

(Plate 10, fig. 7)

Dainty as Dresden-china shepherdesses, the delicate pink and white blossoms of the fringed gilia cover the bare spots of grassy mesas with exquisite spring-time bloom. One would not expect so lovely a flower to be a hardy pioneer, but the low spreading plants with thread-like brown stems and dark-green leaves are at their best where there are no competitors for the means of existence. On the other hand, if these become too meagre where the soil is hard and dry instead of sandy, the flowers become pale and dwarfed—at times but three-eighths of an inch across on stems half an inch long, and only one blossom to a plant. Under unusually favorable conditions, a single plant may cover an area five or six inches in diameter and bear a dozen blossoms twice as large as usual.

It is in the morning only that the fringed petals open wide, being tightly furled together at other times. The satiny corollas are white, pale-rose or deep rose-purple, with white centers and yellow throats ringed with dark-purple. They are charming for rock-work or edgings in the unusual garden, and deserve to become more widely known beyond their native limits.

YELLOW GILIA

GILIA AUREA

(Plate 10, fig. 8)

The yellow gilia companions its near relative the fringed gilia, in California, but ventures to travel alone as far eastward as Arizona and New Mexico. It is a tiny plant with branching, thread-like stems and flowers that are usually some dark shade of yellow, but occasionally white or cream-colored. Since the blossoms are closed in the late afternoon, it takes a keen eye to discover the plants among taller growing species.

MOUNTAIN PHLOX

PHLOX DOUGLASI

(Plate 11, fig. 1)

This pretty little phlox spends the summer days in cool mountain air, creeping over gravelly soils and producing masses of rose-purple flowers amid innumerable needle-shaped leaves. It resembles the fringed gilia in leaves and in the habit of forming mats of bloom, but the individual flowers differ in possessing a slight constriction in the tube while the gilia blossoms are open-throated.

Like the gilias, the phloxes are one hundred percent American, but, instead of remaining in the West, they have wandered far and wide over the northern continent—from the Atlantic to the Pacific and from Mexico to Canada. They have also won their way into general garden culture where they are often known as sweet Williams, and many have attracted the attention of gardeners abroad. It is the gorgeous coloring of some that has given to the genus the name of phlox, which means flame.

ALPINE POLEMONIUM

POLEMONIUM CONFERTUM

(Plate 11, fig. 2)

Far beyond timber-line on the summits of the high Sierras and Rocky Mountains, sheltered from wind and sun by granite boulders, the blue blossoms of the alpine polemonium spread their fragrance on the clear cold air. A view of the globe-like clusters of flowers surrounded by graceful foliage is well worth the climb, but it is to be hoped that they will be left undisturbed in their rocky seclusion by those fortunate enough to come upon them.

Plate 11

PHLOX FAMILY

POTATO FAMILY

WATERLEAF FAMILY

1
2
3
4
5
6
7

The polemoniums, like their relatives the phloxes and gilias, are decidedly partial to America, especially the western slope. The resemblance of these three is close and one soon comes to recognize the family features they possess in common.

The plant illustrated is the shade-form found in rock-clefts on the highest peaks and is sometimes regarded as a distinct species (Polemonium speciosum).

LOW POLEMONIUM

Polemonium humile

(Plate 11, fig. 3)

Seeking the moist shade of spruce, fir or lodgepole pine, the low polemonium often covers the ground with prettily cut leaves on low stems, and pale-blue or white flowers in graceful clusters. Anyone who has seen the creeping polemonium (Polemonium reptans) of open woods in the East will quickly recognize the two as being closely related.

Yellow-flowered polemoniums are not as satisfactory for growing in the garden as the many blue-flowered species are, but all are easily cultivated. Jacob's ladder (Polemonium cæruleum) has long been a favorite in old-fashioned gardens, for the sake of its attractive foliage and large blue bell-shaped blossoms. A horticultural form of the low polemonium is one of the finest in cultivation. It sometimes produces as many as a score or more large bright-blue flowers in a cluster often six inches wide and deep.

POTATO FAMILY

Solanaceæ

The potato family is an unusually large one estimated to comprise more than two thousand species, which are well represented in temperate regions but abound especially in the tropics. In the ranks of this host are to be found plants that are purely ornamental as well as many that are valuable as the source of food and drugs.

The latter are the well-known narcotics, belladonna, mandragora, stramonium, henbane and nicotine.

The red sap of belladonna was formerly used by women in Italy as a cosmetic, whence the name which means beautiful woman. The plants are poisonous in all their parts and, although of restricted range in this country, have proven fatal to children who have been attracted by the red berries and purple blossoms. Stramonium also is a source of danger. This is the thorn-apple or Jimson-weed which thrives in waste places throughout the country and tempts children to blow bubbles with its large trumpet-shaped blossoms or to play with the prickly pods full of black seeds. It is the seeds that yield the highly narcotic drug and children have paid the full penalty for eating them. In early days, magicians and sorcerers were accustomed to make use of both stramonium and mandragora in order to produce fantastic visions and hallucinations in their dupes, while thieves found them useful as a means of stupefying their victims.

The name of the tomato means wolf-peach and probably refers to its supposedly poisonous nature. This suspicion lasted a long time and even today there are some Europeans who are afraid to eat tomatoes. Another familiar name was that of love-apple, based upon the supposed effect of eating the fruit. It may be that some of the earlier wild species recommended as love-potions produced visions and hallucinations as the mandragora did. Today the tomato is especially recommended for the sake of the vitamine it contains.

Other contributions of the potato family to the diet are red pepper, egg-plant, wonder-berry and potato, while of the garden plants and ornamentals mention should be made of the petunia, cestrum, salpinglossis, butterfly-flower (Schizanthus) and Chinese lantern, the inflated vermilion calyx of which persists for a long time as a diminutive paper lantern.

The potatoes claim the waterleafs and morning-glories as next of kin. They differ from the latter in forming many-seeded in place of few-seeded fruits, and from the former in the two-celled ovary.

BLUE NIGHTSHADE

Solanum umbelliferum

(Plate 11, fig. 4)

The shallow corollas of the blue nightshade are prettily ruffled and pointed where the petals join together; they vary in color from pale lavender-blue to deep-purple, with occasional albinos. An effective contrast is supplied by the cone of yellow stamens in the center, surrounded by green spots edged with white. The color-scheme is charming in the spring and summer when the loose clusters of buds and full-blown or half-opened flowers adorn the bushy plants, and again later when these are replaced by bright green or purple berries.

This blue nightshade is partial to the gulches and canyons of the hill country in California, but crosses the line into Nevada as a slightly different form (Solanum xanti). It is not poisonous, although sometimes called blue-witch, probably because of the evil reputation of some of its relatives. Other members of the group have narcotic properties and it is due to this that the name of solanum, which means solace or quieting, is given them.

Unfortunately many a solanum may be safe and trustworthy at one time and a menace to life and health at another—playing the part of Dr. Jekyll and Mr. Hyde in plant society—so that one must be on guard where they are concerned. One of the most treacherous is the black nightshade (Solanum nigrum) which grows all over the world in damp or shady places, but especially in cultivated and waste ground near towns. It has very small white flowers and shiny black berries that are frequently used in pies and preserves. Since they are poisonous when green, care should be taken to see that they are thoroughly ripe and well-cooked before being eaten. The leaves are sometimes used in tropical regions as a pot-herb, but they too require adequate cooking. Under cultivation, the black nightshade produces unusually large and handsome fruits that have won considerable notice under the name of wonder-berries. The black nightshade (Solanum douglasi) of coastal California and the deserts may be distinguished by its perennial habit and larger flowers. These are about three-fourths of an inch across, flat and shaped like five-pointed stars.

Probably the most highly prized and best-known solanums are the common potato (Solanum tuberosum) and the egg-plant (Solanum melongena, var. esculentum); the latter is esteemed for its large edible fruits and the former for its tubers. The green berries of the potato are actively poisonous and the tubers may be also when showing a greenish tinge in the skin, as well as when actively sprouting. The scarlet berries of the bittersweet (Solanum dulcamara) are poisonous at all times and are a source of danger to children who are attracted by their bright colors.

TREE TOBACCO

NICOTIANA GLAUCA

(Plate 11, fig. 5)

Over thirty years ago the tree tobacco, at that time a resident of South America, traveled north and settled down in the Golden State, and today it is as much at home in southern California as any Native Son. From year to year it stakes out claims to more territory, but these do not often conflict with prior real-estate rights, since it is from waste places and roadsides that the tall bending stems, with silvery leaves and trumpet-shaped flowers, make graceful curtsies.

The dried leaves of the tree tobacco are sometimes used for smoking, but the tobacco (Nicotiana tabacum) that is cultivated for this purpose is an annual with large red or rose-colored flowers. The genus is named for a Frenchman, Jean Nicot, who when ambassador to Portugal in the fifteenth century is said to have secured the seeds from Florida and to have presented them to Queen Catherine de Medici, together with a box of powdered tobacco. Since that time, when the queen acquired a taste for the weed, its use has spread to such an extent that it is estimated that today more than eight hundred million people habitually smoke or chew it or take snuff. The effects of this indulgence vary with the individual, but in its pure state nicotine is one of the most virulent of poisons, a single drop sufficing to kill a dog, while smaller animals succumb to but a whiff of the vapor.

The Jimson-weed (Datura meteloides) of the southwestern states and Mexico also possesses virulent narcotic properties and the medicine men of the southern Indian tribes were accustomed to use an infusion of the leaves or roots to produce hallucinations, stupefaction or frenzy when performing their ceremonial rites. This plant is common in southern California, where it redeems the ugliness of waste places with large loose clumps of grayish-green leaves and huge trumpet-flowers, six to eight inches wide, that are dazzling white in the morning but turn to a delicate blue-lavender later in the day.

WATERLEAF FAMILY

Hydrophyllaceæ

Like their near relatives the phloxes, the waterleafs are ornamentals native to North America with the larger number of species on the west coast. Phacelias and nemophilas are grown in many a flower garden and well repay cultivation with masses of foliage and an abundance of bloom over several months.

Both the common and scientific names of the family are drawn from the water-marks on the leaves of the genus Hydrophyllum.

WHISPERING-BELLS

Emmenanthe penduliflora

(Plate 11, fig. 6)

The buds of whispering-bells stand erect, but as the flowers open they bend downward on such slender stalks as to shake in the lightest breath of air. Later in the season the petals become dry and papery, and as the breeze wanders over the hillsides and stirs the pendant blossoms, there may be heard faint, rustling sounds like soft whispers. In this condition the flowers are employed as everlastings in floral decorations, a use denoted by the name emmenanthe, which means everlasting flower.

The plants may be single-stemmed and but a few inches tall in dry situations or much branched and two feet or more high where there is sufficient moisture. They are found frequently on dry open slopes in central and southern California, especially where the chaparral has recently been burned. The seeds are difficult to germinate, seeming to require either wood-ashes, or heat, for they spring up in unusual abundance after fire has swept over the hills.

YERBA SANTA

ERIODICTYON TOMENTOSUM

(Plate 11, fig. 7)

Lovely lilac blossoms blend harmoniously with soft gray foliage on the shrubs of yerba santa and give a characteristic touch to the coastal hills of southern California. The leaves are so very velvety that they furnish the inspiration for both generic and specific names —eriodictyon meaning woolly-net, and tomentosum, covered with a dense white down. The more northern species (Eriodictyon californicum), which occurs on dry hills and lower mountain slopes, from central California to Washington, is similar in general appearance though the leaves are dark shiny green above and downy beneath. They are aromatic and bitter, and their use as a remedy for colds and similar ills gave rise to the name of holy herb among the early Spanish settlers. The Indians also were accustomed to brew the leaves into a tea for fever, and to smoke and chew them as a sort of tobacco.

CUP PHACELIA

PHACELIA PARRYI

(Plate 12, fig. 1)

The royal-purple blossoms of the cup phacelia add their rich tints to the spring verdure of southern California, often covering open places in the chaparral with unbroken masses of color. The flowers are shallower than those of the bell phacelia which wears the same shade of purple, and each petal is ornamented with a cream-colored spot at the base.

The reddish stems are branching, hairy, rather sticky, and grow to a height of a foot or so. The leaves are hairy also and will make a stain on paper, similar to that made by the bee phacelia.

BELL PHACELIA

Phacelia whitlavia

(Plate 12, fig. 2)

The bell phacelia spreads a carpet of purple blossoms over openings in the chaparral of southern California where the moisture still lingers, or loiters in partly shaded foothill canyons until advancing summer suggests that seed-time is near. There is no fragrance to attract the honey-bees, but they hover about, diligently collecting pollen and what nectar they may. The beauty of the graceful flower clusters tempts the vandal, but the reward is a shower of fallen corollas shortly after they are gathered.

A garden plot, sown thick with seeds of the bell phacelia and its varieties, will reward the gardener with a profusion of purple, blue and white blossoms over a long period.

TANSY PHACELIA

Phacelia distans

(Plate 12, fig. 3)

Day by day the close coils of the tansy phacelia slowly unfurl until there is spread a tint of lavender-blue over coastal hill and mesa. On the shore where there is plenty of room and moisture, the plants branch freely and form low growths a foot or more in diameter, while the usual grassland form may be two feet tall and the tiny, starved, drouth form find itself able to produce but one slender stem, two inches in length with a single small group of blossoms at the tip. The entire plant is covered with fine hairs in addition to enough stiff ones to make it rough to the touch and the leaves are very finely cut like those of the garden tansy (Tanacetum vulgare). A closely related species (Phacelia tanacetifolia) bears the name of tansy-leaf in the Latin form and is to be distinguished mainly by longer stamens and a wider distribution. It is also some-

Plate 12

WATERLEAF FAMILY

MORNING-GLORY FAMILY

1
2
3
4
5
6
7

times called fiddleneck because of the coiled inflorescence while the Greek name, phacelia, means curl, and refers to the same characteristic.

The tansy phacelia is such an excellent honey-plant as to have been introduced into Europe in 1832 where it is said to be "literally covered with bees from morning to night." The caterpillar phacelia (Phacelia hispida), which is especially abundant in Ventura county, has been reported as yielding a carload of honey in one season.

BEE PHACELIA

Phacelia grandiflora

(Plate 12, fig. 4)

Burned-over spots in the chaparral belt of southern California are not long allowed to mar the landscape with blackened ruins, for the bee phacelia promptly takes possession and sends up stout, branched stems to a height of two or three feet. From April to May, the buds at the ends of the coiled inflorescences turn from green to white, and, deepening in tint as they unfold, are finally transformed into saucer-shaped blossoms an inch or two in diameter and pale blue-lavender to deep rose-lavender in hue. In the height of the season the tall plants are covered with handsome clusters of showy blossoms, with a delightful fragrance very like that of plum blossoms. This attracts the bees from far and wide to abundant stores of both pollen and nectar.

The bee phacelia is easily grown in the garden, but care must be taken when handling the plants, for the sticky hairs on stem and leaf make unpleasant brown stains on both hands and clothing. This is not only very difficult to remove but is also said to be poisonous.

BABY BLUE-EYES

Nemophila menziesi

(Plate 12, fig. 5)

Reflecting the color of the sunlit heavens, the baby blue-eyes stare up at one from grassy meadows or peep out from the edges of chaparral and woodland where moisture and partial shade protect their delicate stems and leaves from drouth. Lovely as these ethereal blossoms are in their native haunts, they close soon after being picked. They take readily to cultivation, however, and will bloom in a remarkably short time after the seed is sown. In beds and borders, masses of color result, while in shady nooks the fairy-like grace of the individual plants and blossoms is more apparent.

Although nemophila means grove-loving, this species thrives in the sunshine also, as long as there is sufficient moisture in the soil, and may be looked for on valley floors and hillsides throughout California and north to Oregon.

CLIMBING NEMOPHILA

Nemophila aurita

(Plate 12, fig. 6)

The climbing nemophila aspires to greater heights than its sister, baby blue-eyes, and, catching hold of nearby shrub or bush by means of many little hooks on stem and leaf, it clambers over them, mingling its own bright green foliage with theirs and putting forth velvety flowers. These wide-eyed, innocent-looking blossoms are most appealing, but when a cluster is grasped it is as quickly dropped again, for the down-curving hooks on the square stems dig sharply into the flesh like the claws of an angry cat.

The climbing nemophila, true to its name of grove-loving, haunts shady dells and canyons throughout central and southern California. The spotted nemophila (Nemophila maculata) is no less charming than its sisters and is likewise partial to shade, being found in central Californian valleys and meadows of the Yosemite. The white flowers, with a purple blotch at the apex of each petal, are extremely attractive in garden plots.

MORNING-GLORY FAMILY

Convolvulaceæ

Of the morning-glory family, the familiar dwellers in old-fashioned gardens are the morning-glory itself in a large variety of beautiful colors, the fragrant white moon-flower and the crimson and scarlet quamoclits. The sweet potato, although its purple blossoms are very like those of the common morning-glory, is valued for its edible rhizomes which have stored starch. Many of the tropical species yield purgative drugs and our native bindweeds possess the same properties to a less degree. In contrast to the beautiful flowers of most of this group, the dodder has small inconspicuous ones. This is the dishonest member of the family, for it is a parasite that robs its neighbors of food. In a favorable season, it may be seen along the coast, smothering the shrubs of the chaparral with tangled skeins of yellow threads that shine in the sunlight like spun silk.

BINDWEED

Convolvulus arvensis

(Plate 12, fig. 7)

From May until October the close mats of pretty arrow-shaped leaves of the bindweed riot over roadways, ditch-banks and fields. In the late summer there is a profusion of exquisite blossoms—creamy-white or pale-rose—and buds that are more brightly colored, especially along the folds of the spirally twisted corolla. They make extremely satisfactory house bouquets since the leaves keep fresh a long time and the buds continue to open for several days. Moreover, this is one of the few wild-flowers that may be gathered in abundance without fear of protest from the Wild-flower Preservation Society and certainly not from the farmer who considers the bindweed one of the worst of his pests. If allowed to gain a foothold in a field of grain or in the vegetable or flower garden, it not only wins out in the competition for moisture, but twines about its neighbors until they are thoroughly handicapped. This characteristic habit is indicated by the name of the genus, for convolvulus is the Latin for twining.

Two other bindweeds clamber over railroad embankments, fences and shrubs, the one (Convolvulus luteolus) from San Francisco Bay northward, and the other (Convolvulus occidentalis) south from the same point. They are very similar with large flowers, white or cream-color tinted with pink, and resembling morning-glories in shape.

BORAGE FAMILY

Boraginaceæ

The borages belong to the group of nearly related families, the waterleafs, phloxes and morning-glories to be found in all temperate climates and that are notable for ornament rather than usefulness. The most renowned and best loved of these are the fragrant forget-me-not and heliotrope, with hounds-tongue, anchusa, mertensia, comfrey, bugloss and puccoon less well-known. Among these are several that were used in the very early days for the diseases that seemed to be indicated by the appearance of the plant. Thus, the lungwort was reputed useful in diseases of the lungs, since the mottled character of the leaves suggested such a use; the viper's bugloss was believed to be indicated for snake bites because of the coiled cluster of flowers, and the puccoon or pearlwort was assumed to be good for dissolving bladder-stones because of the hard pearl-gray seeds. This method of prescribing remedies was called "the doctrine of signatures" and had a great vogue until comparatively recent times.

FIDDLE-NECK

Amsinckia intermedia

(Plate 13, fig. 1)

Of the coast borages, fiddle-neck is one of the prettiest at its best, though the bristly herbage and the dropping of the bright-orange corollas as the seeds mature, give a ragged effect to the plants when massed. The individual blossoms are attractive in color and shape and interestingly arranged in a closely coiled inflorescence which unwinds as the flowers open successively along the axis. It is easily seen from the shape of some of these clusters whence comes the name, fiddle-neck. There are several similar species in the coast region that are difficult for the amateur to distinguish, but easy to recognize as close relatives at least. The harsh, rough foliage of all is much relished by grazing animals—mules and donkeys seeming especially to enjoy having their palates tickled by the prickly herbage.

The popcorn flower (Plagiobothrys nothofulvus) is a closely related species that springs up abundantly in burned areas along the coast from southern California to Washington. So freely do the plants blossom after a fire that the early Spaniards called the flowers snow-flakes, while others use the name popcorn flower.

FORGET-ME-NOT

Myosotis sylvatica

(Plate 13, fig. 2)

The forget-me-not is a charming little foreigner that has been brought over from Europe and placed under cultivation in this country. Whether massed in the garden or running wild through the redwood forest, the turquoise-blue blossoms stand without a rival in sheer loveliness of color and delicacy of fragrance. Tiny yellow spots at the opening of the corolla enhance their beauty and also serve to guide the bee to the nectar within.

The forget-me-not (Myosotis palustris) of the eastern coast looks very like this western species. It too is a native of Europe as is also the turncoat forget-me-not (Myosotis versicolor) with flowers that turn from yellow to blue and finally to violet in the course of their development.

In contrast to some flowers whose names are legion, the forget-me-not is called such in many languages, and each nation has a legend to explain its origin. In German fairy-lore, it is regarded as the source of good luck for which one should not forget to be grateful. There is also a German tale of a knight who lost his life in fulfilling the request of his sweetheart that he secure for her the blossoms floating past on the stream. As he sank in the swirling waters, his last words to her were: "Forget me not." In Greek mythology, a messenger of the gods was excluded from Paradise because of love for a mortal maiden whom he refused to forsake. Both lovers finally won their way within the gates by planting seeds of the forget-me-not in every nook and corner of the earth.

Plate 13

BORAGE FAMILY

SNAPDRAGON FAMILY

1
2
3
4
5
6
7

A much more primitive story relates, that when Adam was christening each plant in the Garden of Eden, this little blue-eyed blossom, like many a blue-eyed maiden since, paid so little attention to the lecture that it failed to remember what name had been given. On asking to have the information repeated, it was chided for inattention and sternly commanded to "forget not," and as "forget-me-not" it is known to this day.

The forget-me-not has been regarded for centuries as the emblem of eternal friendship and love. It has often formed the motif of engravings on friendship rings and in the fourteenth century was embroidered on the collars worn by those knights who were faithful to Henry of Lancaster in his exile.

The forget-me-not was formerly employed as a remedy for scorpion stings, since the coiled inflorescence resembled the tail of a scorpion.

MERTENSIA

Mertensia sibirica

(Plate 13, fig. 3)

Where mountain brooks rush noisily down rocky slopes or loiter lazily through grassy meadows, the mertensia hangs out carillons of bell-shaped blossoms—the buds flushing rosily, the full-blown flowers serenely blue. The plants may grow as tall as four or five feet, with long leafy stems arching in graceful curves where the flowers are clustered. Unlike the typical borages which are usually bristly, both stem and leaf are soft and smooth to the touch.

Wherever mertensias grow—whether in the Rocky Mountains of Colorado, the higher Sierra of California or far northward—there is a scene of busy and varied activity as bees and wasps, bumble-bees and humming-birds stop for sips of nectar or loads of pollen and fly away again. The big fellows—wasps and bumble-bees—are indolent but strong. They cling to the outside of the corolla-tube, bite a hole and help themselves to the nectar without so much as a "by your leave." Some of the little bees follow suit and steal a sip through the holes already made while others, more honest, more industrious or less clever, perhaps, cling to the open mouth of the flower, upside down, and, pushing their heads within the tube, suck their fill. Some of the small bees are so greedy or so diligent or both, that they do not even wait for a blossom to unfold but force their heads into unopened buds. Still others crawl entirely into the flower, cling to the stamens, and while eagerly sipping the nectar at the base of the corolla, scrape pollen so vigorously with the hind-legs that it flies out of the tube. Meanwhile, tiny beetles with long horns crawl around inside the blossoms, eating pollen and scattering some of the left-over grains onto the stigma, and humming-birds hover on rapid wings as they dart from flower to flower.

Mertensia is blessed with many names, none of them any prettier than this Latin one which is formed from the name of a botanist, Mertens. The eastern mertensia (Mertensia virginica) is called both Virginia cowslip and bluebell, but since it is neither a cowslip (Primula) nor a bluebell (Campanula), these names are both misleading and meaningless.

SNAPDRAGON FAMILY

Scrophulariaceæ

The snapdragons represent the third great step of advance in the line of development from buttercups to the mints, and although the shapes which the corolla assumes within the limits of the group are of varying degrees of irregularity, it is practically always a distinguishing ear-mark. The family is a remarkably large and beautiful one which shuns both the heat of the equator and the cold towards the poles, but appears in great abundance in all temperate parts of the earth. It comprises herbs, shrubs and trees; aquatics and marsh-plants; wild-flowers of woodlands, plain and mountain, while many are prime favorites of the garden and greenhouse. Of these mention should be made of the pentstemon, speedwell, mullein, snapdragon, toad-flax, collinsia, slipperwort and monkey-flower, while the foxglove is famed in addition to its beauty as the source of digitalis, an invaluable heart-regulator.

The name of the foxglove is intriguing since it seems to have no significance when taken at its face value, but the significance becomes clearer when it is remembered that the word glove is derived from the Norwegian "gleow" which means music and in a different form is found in the word glee-club. The cluster of bell-shaped blossoms of the foxglove bears some resemblance to an early musical instrument which consisted of a ring of bells hung on an arched support. The name thus translated means fox-music instead of the glove of the fox, the connection of this animal with the music being merely fanciful.

BLUE COLLINSIA

Collinsia grandiflora

(Plate 13, fig. 4)

The blue collinsia is especially lovely when massed on shady slopes, the lavender and blue of the two-toned corollas producing an unusual color effect, especially if supplemented by the pink of the rose-colored variety here and there in the mass. This species of collinsia may be found in the mountains from central California to British Columbia, but is easily grown in gardens and will bloom early in the spring if the seeds are sown in the fall. Since the plants rarely grow more than a foot tall and blossom abundantly, they are especially suited to borders.

PINK COLLINSIA

Collinsia bicolor

(Plate 13, fig. 5)

Whether covering shaded banks with tier upon tier of delicately tinted blossoms or filling open places with masses of rose-lavender and white, the pink collinsia is one of the loveliest of spring bloomers. It is often called Chinese houses, since the arrangement of the flowers in crowded circles at intervals along the stem suggests the successively flaring roof-lines of these structures, especially if the stem is unbranched as it commonly is in the shade. In open sunny spots, the plants are apt to be more robust and branching and the flowers take on deeper shades of rose-purple in the lower lip and pale-lavender in the upper one.

Moist situations in the hills and lower mountains of western California may be entirely masked in April and May with these charming blossoms. Under cultivation there are five or six well-marked color-varieties, some of which are pure white, while others are variegated with spots or stripes of different colors.

OWL-FLOWER

Orthocarpus purpurascens

(Plate 13, fig. 6)

Crowded in open spots in the foothills the owl-flowers form sheets of rose-purple, or supply individual touches of color when scattered through the grasses. Not only are the blossoms gay with magenta, yellow and white, but the leafy bracts in between them are crimson or purple-tipped. The curving shape of the upper lip of the corolla and the markings of white and yellow on the lower one may readily be likened to an owl's hooked beak and unblinking eyes. Since this plant belongs to a family far removed from that of the clovers, the usual name of owl-clover is misleading and should be discarded in favor of that of owl-flower. Another owl-flower (Orthocarpus densiflorus) which is common along the coast of California, is paler in tint and more feathery in appearance.

CREAM-SACS

Orthocarpus lithospermoides

(Plate 13, fig. 7)

Cream-sacs is next of kin to the owl-flower and both are loyal Californians, the latter preferring the southern part of the state while the former ventures further north. The blossoms are entirely bright-yellow, the very much inflated lower lip forming a pouch that suggests the name commonly used. A paler yellow companion (Orthocarpus erianthus) trims its sulphur-colored flowers with purple and white and is thus easily distinguished.

YELLOW MONKEY-FLOWER

Mimulus luteus

(Plate 14, fig. 1)

In a land where a limited rainfall occurs only during the cooler seasons, fields and hillsides become brown and dry during the summer months, and flowers are then to be sought only in shady nooks or where moisture lingers in brook-bank and bog. The creeping roots of the yellow monkey-flower enable it to spread widely in such places during the spring and to continue to bloom profusely far into the summer. From California to Alaska and east to the Rockies, the cheery yellow blossoms, freckled with maroon spots, grin impishly up at one as once did the mimics of the Roman stage for whom they were named. Children love to punch the throat and watch the mouth open, apparently in hilarious laughter, and to touch the sensitive stigmas with pencil or finger-tip, fascinated by their prompt closing together under the impact.

In a favorable spring-time, the branching plants of another yellow mimulus (Mimulus brevipes) flower so freely that the hillsides of southern California take on a uniform golden tint. The corollas lack markings and the foliage is sticky and hairy. Still another species (Mimulus primuloides), often found in mountain meadows of the Yosemite, is a dwarf with rosette leaves and dainty golden blossoms.

For growing in the garden, there are strains of the yellow mimulus (Mimulus luteus) that are gaily mottled and variegated with contrasting colors, while the musk-plant (Mimulus moschatus) combines scented foliage with pale-yellow flowers. A near relative, the snapdragon (Antirrhinum) is also a prime favorite in gardens, not only because of its remarkable range and combination of colors, but also on account of the wealth of bloom and the fanciful form of the flower. The inflated lower lip which closes tightly against the upper one and opens wide under pressure at the side of the throat, has a curious resemblance to the mythical dragons of former days and lacks only fangs and a fiery breath to complete the illusion. Simple folk in many countries are so impressed by this that

Plate 14

SNAPDRAGON FAMILY

1
2
5
3
6
4

they attribute supernatural influences to the plant, believing that it is able to render charms and maledictions harmless.

SCARLET MIMULUS

Mimulus cardinalis

(Plate 14, fig. 2)

The petals of poppies are like crinkled crepe or lustrous satin; everlastings take on a durable texture like stiff paper while pansies and the scarlet mimulus clothe themselves in velvet. The rich warm-red of these velvety corollas blends to yellow in the throat which is marked with crimson guide-lines. The turning backward of the lobes makes all the more evident the unusual length of the stamens, so well-adapted to depositing pollen on the humming-birds which favor these crimson long-tubed blossoms.

Swampy places and streamways in California and Oregon and as far east as Arizona, may be made gay with the bright flowers on these dark-green plants. They are the delight of the home gardener, for the bright blossoms appear the first year from seed.

PINK MIMULUS

Mimulus lewisi

(Plate 14, fig. 3)

Monkey-flowers of yellow or scarlet may grin widely up at one from swamp and streamway; buff, orange or vermilion ones signal from hill-slope and valley; but it is in mountain meadows that the pink mimulus is to be sought. The blossoms are large and showy, rose-pink with yellow throats, and are borne in pairs on slender stalks. The plants are perennial and should be looked for in damp ground and along stream-banks in the Selkirks, the entire length of the Sierra Nevada and as far east as Montana and Utah. The dwarf mimulus (Mimulus fremonti) forms dense low-growing mats, especially where the chaparral of southern California has been burned, and these may be so thickly covered with bloom as to give a tint of rose-color to the blackened soil. The flowers are rose-purple with crimson throats and are somewhat smaller than those of the pink mimulus illustrated, and are similarly borne in pairs. The foliage is disagreeably sticky and at close range gives off a faintly unpleasant odor.

BUSH MIMULUS

Mimulus glutinosus

(Plate 14, fig. 4)

Mingled with the chaparral or forming evergreen thickets on rocky banks, the bush monkey-flowers are among the most characteristic features of the coast vegetation of southern and middle California. They are exceedingly variable in both flower and foliage, several being frequently recognized as species. The more southern form, common on dry hills around San Diego, is distinguished by glossy dark-green leaves and dark-crimson flowers of a velvety texture. Northward the blossoms are larger and pale-buff in color, the foliage also being correspondingly lighter green. Between these two extremes many gradations in color and tint occur—such as salmon, orange, vermilion and rich red. In all these forms, the foliage is smooth and sticky, the edges of the corolla-lobes are scalloped and the stigmas sensitive, the two flat lobes closing almost with a snap at the slightest touch.

Whatever variety may be chosen for garden culture, the shrubs are ornamental and the blossoms satisfactory for cutting, since they last for many days.

PEDICULARIS

Pedicularis ornithorhyncha

(Plate 14, fig. 5)

The dark rose-purple clusters of oddly shaped blossoms of pedicularis form fascinating groups in boggy mountain meadows of Washington and Oregon, but especially on Mount Rainier. The plants rarely grow over six inches tall, the purplish stems springing from a basal cluster of deeply cut leaves and bearing flowers in a compact head at the tip.

Oddly formed as the curved and hooded corollas appear at

first sight, those of the elephant-head (Pedicularis grœnlandica and P. attollens) are even more fantastic, the upper lip being extended into a long curved beak very like the elephant's trunk. Both species are rose-purple in color and dwell in moist mountain meadows, the former preferring somewhat higher altitudes, the latter further distinguished by a dense covering of white hairs. One of the most striking members of the same genus is the tall stout species called Indian warrior (Pedicularis densiflora) which may be found on wooded hillsides from southern California to Oregon. The foliage is finely cut and feathery and the blossoms crimson with purplish bracts. They are borne in a dense spike at the end of a stout stem, a foot or two tall, and are seen to resemble the stiff head-dress of feathers worn by Indian chiefs.

SCARLET PAINTBRUSH

CASTILLEIA MINIATA

(Plate 14, fig. 6)

Where the chaparral is low and open, spots of scarlet-vermilion flash vividly against the dark-green of buckwheat, sage and sumac as the scarlet paintbrush comes into bloom. Not a small part of the bright color is due to the bracts and calyxes which rival the corollas in hue. The plants are always found close to the shrubs upon which they are partly dependent for food, although quite able to take care of themselves by means of their own root-systems and green, food-making leaves, if other sources fail.

Bright red flowers are especially favored by humming-birds, and the scarlet paintbrushes are no exception, although visited occasionally by bees also. The corolla-tube is long and slender with a narrow slit through which the visitor must thrust tongue or bill to reach the nectar at the base of the pistil. Sometimes the slit holds the bill of the humming-bird so tightly that it has difficulty in freeing itself. Bees exhibit great individuality in their attempts to find and open this slit. Some are easily discouraged in the face of difficulties and fly away after walking over the flower and eating what pollen grains are to be found on the outside, while others persist until successful.

The name paintbrush seems well chosen since the various species of Castilleia include a nearly complete palette in their range of colors—cream-white, pale-yellow, rose-lavender, rose-purple, orange and shades of red, from vermilion to scarlet. Only the blues are lacking. The paintbrushes are mostly mountain lovers, this scarlet one being found from the foothills almost to timber-line and from southern California to Alaska and throughout the Rockies. The woolly paintbrush (Castilleia foliolosa) is distinguished by its shrubby habit, orange-red tint and preference for the dry hills of California. Several species of Castilleia occur in the Rocky Mountains; a cream-colored one (Castilleia sessiliflora) is common on the prairies and a crimson annual (Castilleia coccinea) often turns the swamps of the East into flame.

CLUSTERED PENTSTEMON

Pentstemon confertus

(Plate 15, fig. 1)

The blue masses of the clustered pentstemon may be glimpsed from afar as they cover mountain slope or meadow in the Sierra Nevada or northern Rockies. On nearer view the stems are seen to be straight and unbranched, with the flowers arranged in crowded circles or whorls, of which the taller individuals in the shade may boast several while the dwarfs of dry soil or high altitudes are able to produce but one at the tip. In some localities the blossoms are creamy-white or pale-yellow, but they may still be recognized by their characteristic grouping.

The name pentstemon is fashioned from the Greek for fifth stamen and refers to the stamen which may be seen lying in the lower part of the throat of the flower. It has lost its ability to produce pollen and now serves to force the bees against the anthers as they enter or leave.

Pentstemons are even more gorgeous and abundant in the Rocky Mountains than on the west coast and two very beautiful ones are frequent on the prairies of the Middle West. One of these (Pentstemon grandiflorus) is sometimes six to eight feet tall and bears lavender flowers two inches long; the other (Pentstemon cobæa) is only a foot or two tall but possesses flowers nearly as large and attractive, pale-lavender in hue.

CLIMBING PENTSTEMON

PENTSTEMON CORDIFOLIUS

(Plate 15, fig. 2)

Pentstemons that climb are as rare as white blackbirds and when to this habit are added flowers of vermilion-red, a color very unusual for this genus, there is a twofold claim to distinction. These bright-red blossoms seem to be borne on many different kinds of shrubs in the chaparral belt of southern California, but closer inspection reveals the fact that they are on long stems that clamber through and over the shrubs. This climbing habit and the shape and color of the flowers have led to their being called honeysuckles, but this is unfortunate since the structure of the pentstemon is very different and the name obscures their true relationship. The sterile filament in the throat of the blossom furnishes a ready means of identifying it as a pentstemon, while the position of the ovary places it on the right-hand branch of the family tree instead of the center one where the honeysuckles are to be found.

SCARLET BUGLER

PENTSTEMON CENTRANTHIFOLIUS

(Plate 15, fig. 3)

Red is the color that challenges the attention the most quickly, whether it be in a flag, a gown or a flower. So it is not strange that the scarlet bugler catches even the fleeting glance by its shafts of color glowing against a dark background of chaparral, where a lesser tint might easily pass unnoticed. The stiff straight stems bear smooth, gray-green leaves and long spikes of drooping red blossoms. The tubes are so long and narrow that many bees are barred from access to the nectar at the base. Humming-birds, however, are quite able to reach it and they may be seen darting about these blossoms as well as those of the climbing pentstemon (Pentstemon cordifolius) and the scarlet pentstemon (Pentstemon

Plate 15

SNAPDRAGON FAMILY

BROOM-RAPE FAMILY

1
2
3
4
5
6
7

bridgesi) of the mountains. This last species strikes root in rocky banks in the Sierra Nevada, from the Yosemite southward, and looks very like the scarlet bugler which grows in warm, dry situations such as stony streamways and on foothill slopes. It is to be found especially in southern California and less abundantly north to Monterey and east to Arizona. The scarlet bugler (Pentstemon barbatus) of the Rockies may be recognized as closely akin to the western species and enjoys the distinction of being already under cultivation.

TINTED PENTSTEMON

Pentstemon heterophyllus

(Plate 15, fig. 4)

As the buds of the tinted pentstemon burst into bloom, they turn gradually from pale-yellow into showy blossoms with inflated rose-purple tubes and turned-back lobes of deep purple-blue. These attractive blossoms are clustered thickly for a distance of eight inches or more at the ends of the long branches and are very striking in full bloom. They will, however, disappoint anyone attempting to gather them into bouquets, for the corollas fall within a day after being picked.

This pentstemon favors dry hillsides of the chaparral belt of southern California and the Coast Ranges while the azure pentstemon (Pentstemon azureus) may be found in similar situations further north. A blue species (Pentstemon lætus), often mistaken for the tinted pentstemon, finds its home in the Sierra Nevada while still another (Pentstemon spectabilis), though similar, is larger in every way and forms huge clumps of leafy stems, sometimes six to eight feet tall with long spikes of handsome purple-blue blossoms.

BUSHY BEARD-TONGUE

Pentstemon antirrhinoides

(Plate 15, fig. 5)

Whether cultivated in the garden or growing wild on warm hillsides of southern California, the bushy beard-tongue is a beautiful shrub, well adapted for decorative purposes. The spreading leafy branches, dotted with bright yellow, oddly shaped blossoms, make charming festoons among the other shrubs of the coastal sagebrush. The unusually wide and gaping throats of the flowers afford a clear view of the sterile fifth stamen, which in this species is thickly bearded with short hairs and suggests an appropriate common name. Nearly all the species of pentstemon are handsome ornamentals that offer a wide range of choice in color, size and general appearance. All are perennial, but some of them may be brought into bloom the first year.

VERONICA

Veronica americana

(Plate 15, fig. 6)

Many a slow-moving streamlet or meadow with wet soil offers a home to the little creeping veronicas with their smooth leaves and loose, spreading clusters of two-toned blue blossoms. These are small circles of pale-blue, so striped with darker lines radiating from the center as to resemble the iris of an eye. As a consequence, they are called cat's-eyes in some parts of England, but the names most commonly used are those of veronica in honor of a saint, and speedwell because of the medicinal virtues of some species.

Tiny blossoms must be content with less important visitors than bumble-bees and humming-birds, unless they band together into communities like those of the clovers and dandelions. Veronicas are glad to welcome the black and gold hover-flies, often enough like honey-bees in appearance to deceive the uncritical. These attractive insects dart from flower to flower, hovering in front of each as though admiring the blossom before alighting to suck the nectar. Their tongues are short and the flat corollas offer easy access to the honey. The two spreading stamens are grasped by the fore-legs and drawn beneath the body of the fly as it clings to them for support. The stigma is placed in such a way as to touch the underside of the insect and pick up pollen in consequence.

Veronicas are widely cultivated and furnish a pleasing variety in both color and flower arrangement. Some are especially effective as hedges and the glossy or glaucous evergreen leaves are unusually decorative. These are natives of New Zealand and must be grown in greenhouses in the colder parts of the country, although in California they are almost ever-blooming and thrive unusually well along the coast.

The moth-mullein (Verbascum blattaria) is a close relative of the speedwell. The plants are very tall and striking along the roadside or in waste fields and are especially ornamental when planted in rows. The flowers are a lovely clear yellow with a curious habit of blooming at two points along the stem, a bud on the upper half opening at the same time as one several inches lower down. Since there are several buds in each cluster, the two series of blossoms seem to chase each other up the stalk. The great-mullein (Verbascum thapsus) is even more stately than the moth-mullein, its impressive height of ten or twelve feet earning it the title of Jupiter's-staff. The flowers of both are similar but the rosette of leaves at the base of the latter are quite woolly with long soft hairs.

BROOM-RAPE FAMILY

OROBANCHACEÆ

The broom-rape family comprises but a very small group of parasites that live upon the roots of green plants. Like all plants that have lost their ability to make food, the green color in stem and leaf is replaced by other hues, and broom-rapes, like Indian-pipes, appear in robes of brown, purple or yellow. Some have lost all but mere vestiges of leaves and consist merely of absorptive organs and flowering stalks. Many are pests of agriculture, and nearly every crop has its own particular hanger-on which drains it of vitality. Alfalfa, clover, hemp, maize, tobacco and beans are all subject to the attacks of different species of the few genera in the family and although the majority dwell in the neighborhood of the Mediterranean Sea, they may be found here and there in north temperate countries.

CANCER-ROOT

Orobanche fasciculata

(Plate 15, fig. 7)

The clustered dull-yellow stems of the cancer-root, hung with ochre-colored blossoms, are neither abundant nor beautiful enough to attract the attention at first, but once noticed, their unusual appearance arouses interest. A total lack of green color introduces them as members of the I. W. W., which in their case must be interpreted as standing for "I won't work," green plants only being workers in the plant-world. Nearby sage and buckwheat or other shrubs furnish sufficient food-stuff in their roots to support these pale beggars attached to them. A swelling at the point of attachment affords the basis for the common name of cancer-root, while the Greek orobanche means vetch-strangler.

MINT FAMILY

Menthaceæ

A formal introduction is scarcely needed to the members of the mint family—that large group of aromatic plants, useful in the household, ornamental in the garden, valuable in medicine and attractive to the bee. It is quite probable, however, that the housewife uses marjoram, thyme, peppermint, spearmint, pennyroyal and sweet basil without a thought as to their origin or place in the plant kingdom, or any idea of connecting the contents of can and package with vari-colored blossoms in the field. The lavender used to ward off harmful insects from linen, woollen and furs, the rosemary in Eau de Cologne, the hoarhound in cough-medicine, the sage in spring tonics and the savories belong in a family circle that girdles the globe. Many of those that are valued primarily for their fragrance or essential oils, are also ornamental and practically every garden boasts a number. The more purely decorative ones, some of which are not so well-known in this country, are the red-flowered sages and lions-ear, blue or purple skull-cap, dragon-head and bugle-weed.

The flowers of the mints are never very large but they have

worked out the problems of insect-attraction, pollination and seed-production so efficiently as to be considered a highly specialized group, far up in the scale of evolution. They may be recognized by their irregularly shaped, two-lipped corolla, the lower lip providing a landing platform for visiting insects, the upper one fashioned like a hood to contain the anthers which are two or four in number. Four nut-like seeds at the base of the corolla-tube are also helpful family ear-marks.

WOOD-MINT

STACHYS BULLATA

(Plate 16, fig. 1)

The bright flowers of the wood-mint charm the discerning eye, as they cluster about the stem like tiny moths or butterflies with rosy heads and gaily speckled wings. The slender plants stand straight and stiff, like small troops of toy soldiers at the edges of copse and woodland—sentinels guarding the entrance to realms of fancy. The soft, wrinkled leaves give forth a spicy fragrance when bruised. They are covered with hairs that sting feebly, somewhat as a nettle does, so that this species is often called hedge-nettle, in spite of the fact that it is not a nettle and is found along woodsy roadsides. The Greek word, stachys, means spike and refers to the way in which the flowers are borne.

The wood-mint grows on low hills of the Coast Ranges and is a pretty, harmless little plant, quite different from a near relative, the hoarhound (Marrubium vulgare). This is an immigrant from Europe, which has escaped from gardens and spread rapidly, taking such complete possession of waste places and pastures as to crowd out all other vegetation and ruin the land for its original purpose. The plants are perennial, with woolly leaves which smell like balsam, and whitish flowers in dense clusters in the axils of the leaves. However, although the hoarhound is considered a most troublesome weed in many parts of California and Oregon, it furnishes one of the chief sources of nectar in the Arkansas Valley in Kansas and portions of Texas. Other parts of the country report it as producing a dark amber honey of strong flavor, which although

Plate 16

MINT FAMILY

1
2
3
4
5
6

esteemed by some, is generally considered inferior to sage-honey. In spite of the abundance of hoarhound on this side of the water, we import more than a hundred thousand pounds to be used in the treatment of colds and dyspepsia and for making hoarhound candy.

MONARDELLA

Monardella villosa

(Plate 16, fig. 2)

The stiffish stems of monardella, with head-like clusters of rose-purple flowers, are partial to the coastal slopes of California, in the shade of thickets or in open places near the sea. The leaves show considerable variation in texture, some being smooth and others quite soft with fine hairs. They also have a pleasant odor like that of pennyroyal, which this species is sometimes called although the true pennyroyals belong to other genera of the mint family.

The mountain monardella (Monardella odoratissima) seeks dry slopes in pine forests of the Sierra, from southern California north to Washington. It has nearly white flowers and very fragrant leaves that are sometimes brewed into a tea, as are also those of the purple monardella (Monardella lanceolata), an annual of the lower hills and roadsides.

All the monardellas are Westerners, but the monardas of the East are so like them as to be easily recognized as close relatives. The horse-mint (Monarda punctata) occupies sandy ground, from New York to Wisconsin and south to Florida and Texas. It has pale, spotted flowers and yields an oil useful in medicine, as well as a clear amber honey. The wild bergamot (Monarda fistulosa) is even more widely distributed, flourishing in meadow and thicket from Ontario to British Columbia and southward to Florida and Arizona, while the bee-balm (Monarda didyma), with brilliant scarlet flowers, is restricted to the East proper. Bumble-bees, butterflies and humming-birds delight in the monardas, but honey-bees and smaller bees are unable to secure the nectar from the long tubes. These are often punctured at the base by robbers in quest of honey and smaller bees are then accessories after the fact.

SKULL-CAP

Scutellaria angustifolia

(Plate 16, fig. 3)

The purple-blue flowers of the skull-cap rise jauntily erect, two by two, on slender leafy stems. The corolla-tubes are paler than the lobes and quite narrow at the base where queer, reddish calyxes, shaped like tiny sun-bonnets, enclose the seeds after the corollas have fallen. A pinch at the base will cause these small boxes to gape widely and reveal their contents. The Latin name scutellaria is derived from the word for little dish and refers to this oddly shaped calyx, as does also the common name of skull-cap.

The plants of this species are small perennials, a foot or two high, often forming loose mats in the Sierra Nevada or purple beds of bloom in moist ground from British Columbia and Montana to southern California. The skull-cap of the Rocky Mountains (Scutellaria resinosa) and that of the prairies (Scutellaria wrighti) are close relatives, but are much more prodigal of their flowers. Still more delicately beautiful are the clusters of another species (Scutellaria tuberosa) which haunts the edges of chaparral burns, especially in the mountains of southern California. Several occur in the East, the most fascinating being the pigmy skull-cap (Scutellaria parvula), with flowers a quarter of an inch long and the tiniest of caps.

PRUNELLA

Prunella vulgaris

(Plate 16, fig. 4)

Bobbing up here and there among the grasses and other herbs of meadow and roadside, the round-topped clusters of the darkest purple prunellas look absurdly like tiny Topsy-heads bristling with curls. Inflorescences with fewer flowers of paler purple or pink are more common but not so striking.

The wide distribution of this little plant, which rarely overtops twelve inches, is worthy of note, since it has traveled from Europe and Asia to this country where it may be looked for in fields, grassy places and woods generally. In the far West, it adapts itself to a range of altitudes, from sea-level to midway up the Sierras. There are no other species of this genus, but the odd little blossoms look superficially enough like the wood-mint and skull-cap to suggest their near relationship.

The names used to designate this member of the mint family testify to the reputation it enjoyed in earlier days as a cure for many ills. Prunella is said to be derived from the German word for sore-throat for which the plant was originally considered a remedy. It is sometimes written brunella but this is an early form of the word.

WOOLLY BLUE-CURLS

Trichostema lanatum

(Plate 16, fig. 5)

The handsome shrubs of Trichostema, with their showy clusters of richly colored, oddly shaped blossoms, resemble escapes from some Persian garden more than natives of western America. The thick covering of fuzzy violet-colored hairs turns the buds into pink balls of wool and gives a velvety texture to the open flowers, so royally purple in hue. Long purple stamens projecting from the hooded upper lip in a coiled group that uncurls as the blossoms mature, give the name of blue-curls to the genus, while the Greek trichostema, derived from the words for hair and stamen, refer to the slenderness of the latter.

Woolly blue-curls bloom in early summer and are to be sought on dry ridges in the chaparral belt of southern California. The crushed leaves give forth a spicy odor very like that of sagebrush. This fragrance is so much more pungent in another species (Trichostema lanceolatum) as to give rise to such names as camphor-weed, vinegar-weed and turpentine-weed. It is also more widely distributed on dry plains and hills in California and Oregon, where it is a common weed in stubble fields and pastures. The leaves have been used by the Indians in an infusion, as a headache remedy and for stupefying fish in streams so that they could be dipped out in baskets. The flowers yield a good quality of very white honey that continues to flow for several hours after the blossoms have fallen to the ground and that granulates quickly—sometimes even before the bees have time to seal the cells. So abundant is the nectar that the vinegar-weed is listed as the best fall honey-plant in California, some regions reporting a yield of tons of honey in a season.

THISTLE SAGE

SALVIA CARDUACEA

(Plate 16, fig. 6)

Holding itself haughtily erect and looking down upon humbler companions with an air of elegant disdain, the thistle sage is a pale aristocrat, clothed in white wool and girdled and crowned with lavender. So arrogant does it seem, indeed, in its fine raiment and unusual beauty, as to merit the term Persian Prince, sometimes bestowed upon it. The leaves at the base of the stem are thistle-like, with spines at the edges and long soft white hairs that dim the green to a grayish tint. Toward the tip of the leafless stem occur successive ball-like clusters of woolly buds with purple points and edgings to the calyxes, together with lavender blossoms of rare beauty. The upper lip is erect, with two fringed and curving lobes; the lower is large and ruffled, edged with white, while the final touch of beauty is given by bright orange anthers. The long stamen filaments are attached to the edge of the lower lip in such a way that when a bee alights they are bent forward and downward until the anthers touch his back.

The thistle sage is a lover of the Southland, where it grows in the dry or sandy soil of valleys and foothills. The seeds are small, but so full of nutriment that the California Indians grind and then boil them into a sort of mush. The purple-blue salvia (Salvia columbariæ), called Chia by the aborigines, has also been extensively used by them. It is almost as strikingly dark as the thistle sage is light-colored—the one being a brunette in the plant-world, the other a blonde. The plants are stiff straight little annuals, rarely over a foot high, with small flowers in dense clusters along the stem, and are quite common on foothill slopes of southern California.

The warm hills and lower chaparral slopes of southern California are also characterized by several shrubby species of Salvia of peculiar charm and much economic importance in their yield of honey. The snow sage (Salvia leucophylla) is very like the thistle sage in coloring and covers the ground with a lovely flush of rose-lavender on gray-green, when in bloom. Peculiar to the San Diego region, especially the Cuyamaca Mountains, one of the most strikingly beautiful of the shrubby salvias (Salvia clevelandi) may also be seen in the Torrey Pines Park, where the coolness permits it to invade the lower altitudes. The dark, purple-blue blossoms, arranged in close clusters along the stem, are of such a striking color and so abundant on the many upright branches, as to challenge instant attention and admiration. The white sage (Salvia apiana) is celebrated for its delicious honey and the flowers are peculiarly adapted to securing pollination by means of honey-bees. They are white or pale-lavender and the shrubs are covered with a fine white down, which imparts a grayish tint to them. The black sage (Salvia mellifera) is also an excellent honey-plant. Its small pale-lavender or white flowers are grouped in compact clusters at intervals along the stiff stems.

The sages which are cultivated as ornamentals comprise many large-flowered blue and scarlet species and varieties, while the common garden sage (Salvia officinalis) is valued for its leaves, which furnish an oil used in modern medicine, or are dried and powdered as a condiment or savory. The ancients esteemed the sage highly for its medicinal qualities, as is seen in the name salvia, which is derived from the Latin word to save.

ROSE FAMILY

Rosaceæ

As the rose has everywhere and at all times been acclaimed "Queen of all the Flowers" by virtue of its sheer loveliness and beauty, so the family to which it belongs must be considered the Royal Family, even though among its representatives there appears now and then a Cæsar or Lucretia Borgia. These princely mur-

Plate 17

ROSE FAMILY

1
2
3
4
5
6

derers may well have used the same prussic acid found in the wild cherry, which deals out a quick and painful death to hungry sheep. This blot on the scutcheon of the rose family, however, may be overlooked in view of the long list of benefits rendered by other members of the group. So well known are these that it is necessary merely to mention their names to call up visions of exquisitely fragrant pink and white blossoms, luscious fruits or toothsome nuts. Here are scarlet strawberries, crimson cherries, purple raspberries, dark-skinned blackberries and thimble-berries, rosy peaches, red, blue or yellow plums, all sorts of apples, pink-flushed pears, almonds, quinces and choke-cherries. As for ornamentals, volumes have been written on the subject of the varieties and culture of the rose itself and societies have been formed of those interested in the subject. Less prominent, but popular also for gardens, are the geums and cinquefoils, spiræas, ninebark, cotoneaster, hawthorn, juneberry and mountain-ash.

YELLOW AVENS

Geum macrophyllum

(Plate 17, fig. 1)

The golden cups of the avens are hidden far from the gaze of passing crowds, and although they descend to sea-level in the North, one must climb higher than 5000 feet elsewhere to view them in their native retreats. These are wet meadows and shaded places in the mountains of North America, whether in California or New Hampshire, Montana or Alaska. The numerous pistils and the stamens attached to the petals indicate that the flower is not the buttercup that it so closely resembles, but a member of the rose family, while the pretty bur-like fruits and odd leaves with the large central leaflet set it apart from its closest relatives. Two of these, the water avens (Geum rivale) and the urban avens (Geum urbanum) are found in the eastern part of the country, though the latter has come originally from Europe. Both have aromatic roots formerly used in tonics and astringents, as well as for brewing a weak tea for invalids in New England. Such uses may be of long standing, since the name geum is derived from Greek words meaning to have a taste. The Latin avens refers to the reputed power of the urban avens to protect from the venom of poisonous reptiles. The credulous-minded of early days felt safe from visits of the devil if the house contained a root of this plant, and they also used it to treat every known disease.

In addition to being valued as a medicine and a charm, the avens appears in architectural designs and patterns toward the end of the thirteenth century. The artist-monk seems to have been especially attracted to it, the graceful three-parted leaf and five golden petals symbolizing to him the Trinity and the five wounds of Christ.

Cultivated geums are desirable for hardy borders and as rock plants; the long plumy fruits of some of these form an additional attraction to the pure-yellow or bright-red blossoms.

PINK-PLUMES

Geum triflorum

(Plate 17, fig. 2)

The triplet blossoms of the pink-plumes are borne in graceful clusters at the ends of slender rosy stems. They are rose-purple and the same bright color tinges the finely cut leaflets also. Cream-colored petals, peeping forth from the cup-like calyx, are in pleasing contrast to the gay body-color and add a touch of daintiness to this charming plant. As the flower matures, the pale, feathery styles lengthen and when the petals fall there is left a plumy cluster attached to the group of seed-like fruits.

Pink-plumes occur frequently in open places in the middle altitudes of the Rockies and less commonly in the Sierra Nevada and Cascade Mountains, from Tahoe northwards, as well as in the northeastern part of the United States.

POTENTILLA

Potentilla gracilis

(Plate 17, fig. 3)

The bright flowers of the potentilla are so like buttercups that one must look closely to discover that they really are tiny yellow roses. They form loose clusters at the ends of slender but stiff branches and thrive best in grassy clearings, borders of forests and similar locations throughout the Sierra Nevada. The long-petioled leaves at the base of the central stem are covered with soft hairs on the upper surface and dense white wool beneath and are usually divided into five leaflets. The common name cinquefoil, frequently applied to the potentillas, is the French for five-leaf. There is a tradition to the effect that whenever a leaf with the unusual number of seven leaflets is found and placed under the pillow, a maiden will dream of the person destined to be her lover. Less fanciful is the Latin potentilla, which means powerful and refers to supposed healing qualities of certain species. Although the leaves and roots are somewhat astringent, they were doubtless quite powerless to remove the pits of small-pox, as country-folk in early England believed. Their faith in the potency of potentilla in the treatment of fevers led to the superstition that since fever is the work of evil spirits, these in turn could be guarded against by hanging the herb in doorways.

The most attractive potentillas for the garden are hybrids, since they bloom freely from spring to autumn and not only produce a large proportion of double blossoms, but exhibit a wide range of brilliant colors. Shades of orange, bright and dark-reds, such as scarlet and maroon, occur pure or may be beautifully marked with yellow bands.

SHRUBBY CINQUEFOIL

POTENTILLA FRUTICOSA

(Plate 17, fig. 4)

Surrounded by soft green leaves, the golden blossoms of this cinquefoil sprinkle low shrubs with yellow stars through the short summer days of the higher altitudes or in the far North. They seek the coolness of Alaska or the boreal and subarctic zones around the world, or climb the mountains to timber-line. Untrue to the name of five-leaf, there may be anywhere from three to seven leaflets in each leaf, the rolled-back margins making them seem even narrower than they actually are, and the under surface so covered with silky hairs as to glisten like hoar-frost in the sunshine. The tiny mound of pistils in the center of the flower and the many stamens attached to the petals tell the traveler that the cinquefoil belongs to the rose family, whether it be found in familiar haunts at home or far away in Europe or Asia. In China the flowers may be white and the leaves shiny beneath, while elsewhere they may be pale-yellow and the leaves silvery-green on the upper surface. The cheery blossoms have no fragrance to attract honey-bees, and no great abundance of nectar, but small bees, bee-flies, and the smaller butterflies seek them out for pollen.

SPIRÆA

Spiræa densiflora

(Plate 17, fig. 5)

The low bushes of spiræa, covered with round-topped clusters of rosy bloom, are not only attractive in their native setting, but are suitable for garden culture as well. Moist rocky slopes of the Sierra Nevada, north and east to the Selkirks and Teton Mountains in Wyoming, are the haunts of this species, while a taller, handsomer one (Spiræa douglasi) prefers roadsides and moist meadows. This is called hardhack or steeple-bush and although the individual flowers of the two species are similar, the clusters of the latter are spire-like instead of round. The name spiræa is derived from words meaning to become spiral and refers to the flexibility of the branches of the species which the Greeks used for twining into garlands. The nearly related chamise (Adenostoma) of California mountains and hills resembles a white spiræa in its large feathery clusters of blossoms. The dark-green heather-like shrubs form the lower part of the chaparral in the southern half of the state.

Spiræas are deservedly popular plants in the garden, since the shrubs are ornamental and the clusters of white or pink flowers showy. Many kinds are cultivated and they should usually be planted quite deeply in good moist soil.

CALIFORNIA WILD ROSE

ROSA CALIFORNICA

(Plate 17, fig. 6)

Amid the profusion of exotic roses that crowd the gardens of the Pacific Coast or clamber luxuriantly over trellis and arbor, the simple wild rose may easily pass unnoticed, but in the open country the golden-hearted pink blossoms cover shrubs and thickets with bloom and fill the air with fragrance. Roadsides, moist meadows and banks of streams, from Lower California to Oregon and from the coast to 6000 feet in the Yosemite, offer the California wild rose favorable situations for growth. The bushes may flower throughout the year at the lower altitudes, but higher up in the mountains they become dwarfed and bloom over a shorter period. The redwood rose (Rosa gymnocarpa) is a smaller-flowered pink species without fragrance that grows in shady woods of the Coast Ranges.

Wild roses are extremely popular with insect-visitors, but though there are some instances in which honey is made from the nectar, the main object of honey-bees is the gathering of pollen. The large group of stamens in the center of the flower offers an abundant supply which is eagerly sought by flies, beetles, and bees of many kinds—mason, leaf-cutting, honey and bumble. Tiny bees tumble about in the pollen, eating hungrily but having no effect on pollination, which is brought about by bumble-bees. Occasionally the generosity of the rose in keeping open house results disastrously, since the beetles sometimes strip the bushes completely of both flowers and leaves. On the other hand, many a bumble-bee has met sudden death in the golden heart of the rose, for it is here that the crab-spider conceals its yellow body and lies in wait, ready to pounce upon the unsuspecting bee. After being stung to death, the victim is dragged over the edge of the flower to the leaves beneath, where it is eaten at leisure.

The name of the rose is derived from the Celtic word for red, but rose-color now denotes a certain clear shade of pink and every color except blue and purple is to be found among the roses. Since these flowers have been cultivated from time immemorial, there are today innumerable garden varieties and forms, and their culture is the subject of voluminous writings. In contrast to the exotic blooms of the hot-house, wild roses have a simple beauty that should grant them a nook in every garden. They are easily grown, need little pruning and are especially adapted to stream-banks and the edges of woods in their natural setting.

All nations, except the Chinese and Japanese, have rendered homage to the rose from the earliest times. The rose gardens of Persia were once famous the world over and a festival called "the feast of the roses" was long held in that country during the period of their blooming. From India comes a tradition as to the discovery of attar of roses. It is said that the favorite wife of a voluptuous sultan, desiring to please her lord, ordered that the bath in the palace be filled to the brim with rose-water. Under the influence of the warm rays of the sun, drops of oil soon collected and floated on the surface of the pool. Thinking that the water had become corrupt, an attendant began to skim off the oil. The globules burst under the process and gave forth such a delightful perfume that the method of preparing attar of roses was suggested.

In Egypt the "bed of roses" is an actuality, for rose-leaves are made into mattresses for people of rank. These luxuries seem also to have been known among the effeminate Grecian Sybarites, for there is a story to the effect that one of them complained that he had not slept well because one of the rose leaves on which he lay had become crumpled beneath him into a hard lump. Both Romans and Greeks made extensive use of the rose in garlands and chaplets and Roman laws were very strict in regulating their use. There is on record a prison sentence of sixteen years imposed upon a man who used a chaplet of roses unlawfully, while another was put into chains for having crowned himself with flowers taken from a statue.

Among modern nations, the rose still reigns Queen of all the Flowers, and a festival of roses during the height of their blooming is an annual event in many places. Throughout the month of May in Italy, it is a national custom to deck the table or oratory with these flowers, and in Salency, France, a rose festival, which was instituted in the sixth century, has been observed until recently.

Up to the end of the sixteenth century, members of the French Parliaments were accustomed to render homage to the rose on the days of their sittings in the great hall during April, May and June. Peers of the realm, dukes and cardinals took turns in seeing that the rooms were strewn with roses and other flowers, in presenting each member with a crown of roses and in offering an entertainment to the president and councilors of the court.

In England the thirty-year struggle between the Houses of Lancaster and York was called the War of the Roses, since the leaders and common soldiers of the latter house were distinguished by emblems of the white rose and the other side wore the red one as its badge. The two Houses were finally united through the marriage of Henry VII of Lancaster to Elizabeth of York and the wars ceased. The descendants of the royal pair continued to look upon the rose as their especial flower and not only does the architecture of the day abound in ornaments derived from its study, but shields, coats-of-arms and coins bear its impress as well.

From earliest times the rose has been clustered about with legend, fairy-tale and superstition. The origin of the red rose is explained as being due to the blood which flowed from Venus' foot when pierced by a thorn, while the tears which she shed on this occasion caused the white rose to spring up. Another legend claims that roses were all originally white and that they became both red and fragrant only after Cupid had spilled a cup of nectar upon them. The rose is considered sacred to Venus, the goddess of love, who seems not always to have been entirely discreet in her amours. To protect her fair name, Cupid, once upon a time, gave a rose to the god of silence as a bribe not to betray the goddess. In this way it has come to be considered the emblem of silence and the saying "sub rosa" or "under the rose" signifies secrecy. The ancients were accustomed to carve the figure of a rose on the ceiling of the dining-room to indicate that everything said in the freedom of social intercourse should be considered as spoken "sub rosa" and therefore confidentially. The Germans of a later day did the same, and in 1526 a rose was placed over confessionals to impress secrecy upon participants.

PEA FAMILY

Fabaceæ

Although related to the buttercups on the one hand and the roses on the other, the peas form a distinctive group, looking like neither, but with flowers that may be recognized at sight, once the marks of family are known. The garden-peas, beans of all sorts, the peanut and indigo, have blossoms built on the same plan as those of the sweet-pea, clover, wistaria, broom, redbud and lupin. There is practically always present the upright "standard" of two petals, fused into a broad banner, two side-petals called "wings" and two narrower ones joined into a little, canoe-like structure—the "keel." Hidden snugly within the keel are ten stamens, closely surrounding a single pod which may develop seeds known to everyone as kidney-beans, lima-beans, navy-beans, or peas, while the pod itself may remain merely a seed-bearing structure or develop into a wax-bean, peanut or something else, according to its nature. The peanut is worthy special notice because of the odd behavior of the seed-pod. Instead of ripening in place, after pollen has been transferred to the stigma and the anthers and petals have fallen, it is carried out at the end of a stalk. This becomes several inches long, and bending downwards, buries the little ovary in the ground, where it ripens into the familiar fibrous-coated shell containing two or three nut-like seeds.

Besides furnishing many of our favorite vegetables, members of the pea family yield drugs, gums, resins, dyes, forage and honey. The nectar is hidden within the keel at the base of the group of stamens. In order to reach it, the bee rests on the two wing-petals, braces its head against the standard, and by pushing vigorously may succeed in depressing the keel far enough to permit the tongue to enter the opening. As the keel is lowered, the stamens are forced out and up against the body, where they deposit the ripened pollen. It takes a comparatively powerful insect to force the keel of many of the pea-flowers downward, with the result that some species have perfected the mechanism for self-pollination to such a degree that it is independent of insects.

In addition to the vast number of wild-flowers of this family, scattered all over the globe, and in all situations from the tropics to the highest mountains, there are many familiar to gardeners, of which may be called to mind the sweet-pea, rattle-box, a great variety of lupins, locust, acacia, wistaria, laburnum, broom, redbud, bauhinia, parkinsonia, honey-locust, mimosa and albizzia.

CRIMSON SWEET-PEA

Lathyrus splendens

(Plate 18, fig. 1)

Of the wild sweet-peas, none is more beautiful than the crimson sweet-pea of southern and Lower California. The magnificent flower clusters, enthroned on the shrubs and bushes of the chaparral, well merit the term "Pride of California" applied to them. The long, vine-like stems clamber to a height of eight or ten feet, supporting themselves on nearby shrubs, among whose branches the loose clusters of large crimson blossoms are half-concealed, or fully revealed on their summits. If left unprotected, it is quite likely they will eventually be exterminated by the thoughtless gatherers of wild flowers, but they are easily grown from seed and will reward the home gardener with a profusion of early bloom on fence or trellis.

The pink sweet-pea (Lathyrus alfeldi) is sometimes mistaken for the crimson sweet-pea, especially when wearing the deeper tones of color which shade into the reds. It is much more common and is to be found frequently in the foothills of southern California. The garden sweet-pea (Lathyrus odoratus) completes the trio of beautiful blossoms which are closely akin. Bees are attracted by its gay colors and sweet perfume, but only the strongest leaf-cutting bees are able to get at the nectar by depressing the keel of the flower. Honey-bees have learned that they are too weak to do this and rarely alight on the blossoms, although repeatedly stopping to examine them, and some bumble-bees steal the honey through the opening left between the standard and the wings.

Plate 18

PEA FAMILY

1
2
3
4
5
6
7
8

PALE SWEET-PEA

Lathyrus vestitus

(Plate 18, fig. 2)

The pale sweet-pea charms with its delicate violet and rose coloring, rather than challenges admiration with a striking beauty. Like the crimson sweet-pea, it clambers over the shrubs of the chaparral, but it is more common and may be found much farther northward. The flowers turn yellowish as they fade. Honey-bees have learned that these are old flowers without nectar and never visit them.

Sweet-peas are not fond of mountain-climbing, but a dull white species (Lathyrus sulphureus), which turns yellowish-brown with age, may be found as high as the lower part of the pine belt in the Sierra. A close relative (Lathyrus sativus), the white vetch of Europe, is used as a food by both man and beast, but causes paralysis of the muscles if partaken of too freely. Since the poison is dissipated by heat, the peasants are accustomed to mix the ground seeds with wheat-flour and boil this before eating.

MEADOW LOTUS

Lotus oblongifolius

(Plate 18, fig. 3)

The pale-yellow and white flowers of the meadow lotus are to be found occasionally along mountain streams at low altitudes or more abundantly in moist grassy places around mountain springs, where the stems become tall and slender. This form is the one illustrated and is considered a variety. It may be looked for in the Sierra Nevada and North Coast Ranges below 7,000 feet.

The name lotus is the classical name which has been applied to widely differing plants. The lotus of the Nile is a water-lily (Nymphæa), as is also the East Indian lotus (Nelumbium). The jujube-tree (Zizyphus lotus), celebrated from ancient times for its pulpy fruits, is also called lotus though belonging to the buckthorn family, which is far removed from either the water-lilies or the peas.

VELVET LOTUS

LOTUS AMERICANUS

(Plate 18, fig. 4)

The velvety-soft gray-green masses of the velvet lotus, dotted with small shell-pink blossoms, clothe fallow-fields and roadsides with verdure, where dry soil may be a barrier to more exacting plants. It grows so readily throughout the arid belt of the foothills as to be utilized in late summer for forage. When found at the higher altitudes, such as the floor of the Yosemite, the plants become dwarfed and the foliage less hairy, but even here it is abundant and daintily attractive.

The velvet lotus boasts many names, being known in the eastern manuals by the awkward one of "prairie bird's-foot trefoil" and in some of the western ones as "Spanish clover" and "Dakota vetch." All of this is in spite of the fact that it is neither a clover (Trifolium) nor a vetch (Vicia) and is found widely distributed in dry soil throughout the Middle and Far West.

HAIRY LOTUS

LOTUS STRIGOSUS

(Plate 18, fig. 5)

Wherever the grasses of foothills and plains in the South become sparse or are lacking, the bright green mats of the hairy lotus often find a foothold and cover the bare ground with trailing stems and bright-yellow blossoms. These turn red as they fade and as a result honey-bees are saved fruitless attempts to seek nectar in the old blossoms. As a rule the slender stems are but a few inches tall, but such plants as venture in among the nearby grasses and are shaded by them, stretch up higher and become more or less erect.

BUSH LOTUS

LOTUS SCOPARIUS

(Plate 18, fig. 6)

Green, gold and orange are the colors of the long narrow flower-clusters of the bush lotus, the slender curving branches of which twine and intertwine into low shrubs. The bright-yellow of the newly opened blossoms turns to orange and finally to orange-red, bending somewhat downward on their stalks as they fade. Bees hovering about in search of nectar alight unerringly on the fresh flowers, for they have learned by experience that the drooping red ones have no honey left.

In the spring, the shoots of the bush lotus are so leafy and tender that they are browsed by cattle, sheep and deer. Later in the season the branches become hard and wiry and form clumps of half-woody stems. They are found everywhere on dry mesa and hillside, and clothe the ground after a fire with a characteristically dense tangle. The flowers bloom from June to September and yield an abundant supply of honey that is considered especially excellent when mixed with that from the sages.

CHAPARRAL-PEA

Pickeringia montana

(Plate 18, fig. 7)

The chaparral-pea is distinguished by flowers of an unusual shade of purple—and by spiny crooked branches, which form a dense thicket where sufficiently abundant, or mingle with other shrubs of the chaparral of California. The stiff plants grow to a height of three to eight feet and the pretty pea-shaped flowers are borne near the ends of the prickly branchlets.

ALFALFA

Medicago sativa

(Plate 18, fig. 8)

Vast oases of rich green in an arid landscape, the humming of myriads of restless bees, whiffs of a honey-sweet fragrance, borne on the warm wind—such is alfalfa under irrigation. In the Middle West, when left to Nature's whims as to rain and heat, the yield is variable, the bees are capricious and the honey less to be depended upon. West of the Missouri River, good crops of honey and forage are often obtained under natural conditions, but in many localities east of the Mississippi the flowers may lack nectar completely. It is only in the great irrigated sections where sufficient moisture is available for the roots and warm dry air for the leaves and flowers, that this Old World plant yields sometimes as many as five forage crops a season and hundreds of tons of honey.

Butterflies and honey-bees steal the nectar through a gap between the petals, and leave to the sturdy leaf-cutting bees the job of securing it by depressing the keel of the flower and transferring the pollen.

Alfalfa has been known as a valuable forage plant for nearly twenty centuries. The name medicago is derived from the country Medea east of the Mediterranean, while that of alfalfa is from the Arabian words for best fodder. From its far eastern home alfalfa has traveled west across Europe into England and thence, about the middle of the nineteenth century, to this country, where it has steadily grown in favor as a cultivated crop. In addition to its value as a source of hay and honey, it is one of the best legumes for enriching the soil.

Such an experienced traveler is not apt to stay within the bounds set for it by cultivation and as a consequence alfalfa may be found growing wild from coast to coast. The dainty flowers form attractive clusters, varying in tint from pale blue-lavender to dark purple-blue. The seed-pods are queer little spirals which look somewhat like a snail's shell. This resemblance is so striking in the pods of the European species (Medicago scutellata) that they are called "snails" and put into salads and soups by practical jokers.

Another successful little immigrant from Europe is the bur-clover (Medicago hispida), known by its tiny yellow flowers and especially by its odd bur-like pods. These are twisted into several flat spiral coils which are prettily marked with ridged reticulations and armed with hooked prickles on the edges of the coils. As a consequence of the latter, the bur-clover pods are so well adapted to catching hold of nearby objects that they have traveled all over the world and set up families and colonies of plants wherever waste places offer proper growing conditions.

The bur-clover is an excellent forage and honey plant, as are also the nearly related true clovers. The white clover (Trifolium repens) is the most important honey plant of North America, while the red clover (Trifolium pratense) produces cattle fodder as well as honey. This clover is so dependent upon bumble-bees for pollination and consequent seed-production that the farmers of New Zealand were unable to grow it successfully until bumble-bees, which had been unknown to the islands up to that time, were introduced.

It is uncertain whether the honor of being the original Irish shamrock be awarded the black medic (Medicago lupulina), the white clover (Trifolium repens) or the wood sorrel (Oxalis). All possess the arrangement of three leaflets into one leaf, which was considered by St. Patrick to illustrate the doctrine of the Trinity. It is the clover-leaf however, that appears in the pack of playing cards as the suit of clubs.

HARLEQUIN

Lupinus stiversi

(Plate 19, fig. 1)

Dame Nature must have been in a daring mood when she colored the harlequins yellow and pink, for this combination of colors in a flower is as unusual as it is effective. The standard petal waves a banner of bright yellow while the wings and keel are gaily rose-pink. It is these brilliant and contrasting colors, combined with the jaunty air of the blossoms, that remind one of merry Harlequin of pantomime fame.

Harlequins are not inclined to leave their comfortable homes in the warm sandy or gravelly spots in the mountains and never travel from the western slopes of the Sierra Nevada or the few favored localities in the Coast Ranges. Where the forest is open and the shade light, the ground may often be completely covered with the branching leafy plants which come into bloom in early summer and soon mature.

The flowers have no nectar, but possess an abundance of pollen and an interesting mechanism for loading it during the visits of the

Plate 19

PEA FAMILY

1
5
6
2
3
7
4

bees. The ten stamens lie enclosed in the keel, but the five outer ones ripen first, discharge their pollen within the keel and then wither. When the bee alights on the flower, the other five stamens are stimulated to act as a piston which pushes the pollen out of its prison on to the insect.

The name lupinus, applied to this large group of flowers in the pea-family, has been fashioned from the Latin word for wolf, since the ancients believed that lupin plants destroyed the fertility of the soil very much as a wolf destroys its prey.

BLUEBONNET

Lupinus succulentus

(Plate 19, fig. 2)

Although not covering such vast areas as do some other lupins, the bluebonnets of southern California are individually attractive, as they thriftily take root in heavy clay soils and put forth spikes of dark-blue flowers. As the blossoms age, there appears a crimson spot at the base of the standard which enhances the beauty of the inflorescence at the same time that it conveys information appreciated by the bee in his efforts to gather the greatest amount of honey in the shortest space of time.

Among the many flowers that cover burned-over hillsides in southern California with rainbow colors, none are handsomer than the wand lupin (Lupinus formosus), with long spikes of charming blossoms—pale lavender to blue-purple—arising from clumps of beautiful gray-green foliage. Pure white forms contrast exquisitely with the tinted blues, and a honey-sweet fragrance attracts the bees from far and wide.

DWARF LUPIN

Lupinus nanus

(Plate 19, fig. 3)

The flowers of the dwarf lupin catch the eye of both man and insect the more quickly because of the purple-dotted white spot which contrasts with the bright blue of the petals. This is placed at the base of the standard, above the opening that leads to the nectar, so that bees are able to reach the latter without loss of time. These fragrant blossoms form stretches of purple here and there on the grassy hills of central California.

Under cultivation, the dwarf lupins put forth an abundance of flowers that are especially well adapted to borders and masses, and are all the more attractive because of frequent variations in color.

BEACH LUPIN

Lupinus chamissonis

(Plate 19, fig. 4)

The shrubby plants of the beach lupin, with their silvery-green leaves and large spikes of blue flowers are a frequent sight near the sea, where they form clumps on the sand-dunes along the shore. The nature lover must be content to recognize this lupin by these ear-marks since the blossoms vary so greatly in size and color as to tempt the specialist to split the species into several that can be recognized by him alone.

The showy fragrant flowers bloom very nearly throughout the year and may be found in their sandy homes from southern California to Oregon.

YELLOW LUPIN

Lupinus arboreus

(Plate 19, fig. 5)

Shifting sand-dunes near the coast may be held in check by the long roots of the yellow lupin shrubs, while above ground splendid spikes of bright blossoms perfume the air. In the spring the sandy hills of the coast, from central California southward, may be unbroken masses of these plants which are strikingly beautiful in form and produce a profusion of bloom.

The individual flowers are large and showy, resembling closely those of a related genus (Thermopsis montana) which is an herbaceous perennial in the mountain meadows of Oregon, Washington and the Rockies. A popular shrubby garden plant that is also closely akin is the broom (Genista) with canary-colored flowers.

VETCH

Vicia americana

(Plate 19, fig. 6)

Rose-purple and pale-pink, the butterfly blossoms of the vetch perch saucily on wayside bushes which have been festooned by its trailing stems and curling tendrils. The pretty little leaflets are numerous and dark-green and differ so much in various localities that varieties have been named accordingly. They grow readily in moist soil across the continent and may easily be confused with some species of sweet-pea, since the flowers are very similar in outward appearance. One must look carefully at the stigma within the keel to see whether the hairs form a tuft, as in the vetches, or extend in a line down the style, as in the sweet-peas.

The name vetch is from a Latin word signifying to bind together and refers to the tendrils by means of which the stems clamber over other plants. The flowers are rich in nectar, which is stolen by the bumble-bees or made into large quantities of honey by the honey-bees. The hairy vetch (Vicia villosa) is especially rich in honey and is also grown in British Columbia as a cover-crop. The spring vetch (Vicia sativa) is used for the same purpose in California, but although it is not the equal of the hairy vetch in the production of honey it is even more nutritious than hay or any other herbage. Other varieties of vetch are also cultivated for forage, and the horse-bean (Vicia faba) has long been utilized as food for both man and beast.

SCARLET LOCO

Astragalus coccineus

(Plate 19, fig. 7)

As rare as it is brilliant, the scarlet loco belongs more to the desert than to the coast, although it ventures within sight of the latter on the mountains of southern California. The low-growing plants combine silvery-gray leaves with gay blossoms into a color-scheme as unique as it is beautiful. Outside of its intrinsic charm, the scarlet loco is interesting because of its connection with relatives notorious for the enormous losses they have occasioned stockmen. These are called crazy-weeds because of the odd behavior they induce in cattle which graze upon them, and the Spanish term locoed similarly refers to abnormal mental behavior. The danger to range-stock is due not so much to the virulence of the poison lurking in loco-weeds as to the fact that it is a habit-forming drug and animals that acquire a taste for it indulge their appetites to their destruction. Some species of loco-weed are harmless, but the purple loco (Astragalus mollissimus) of Texas and New Mexico, the blue loco (Astragalus diphysus) of Arizona and the Southwest, and the white loco (Aragalus lamberti), which covers vast areas of the plains east of the Rockies, are the worst offenders.

The name astragalus is derived from a word meaning vertebra and refers to the squarish form into which the row of seeds of some species have been squeezed. Other species (Astragalus crotalaria and A. oocarpus) have pods so greatly inflated that they make excellent "poppers."

STONECROP FAMILY

Crassulaceæ

The members of the stonecrop family are usually succulent plants with a watery juice that is astringent and has been used either as a refreshing drink or as an emollient. The fleshy leaves serve to permit these plants to remain green and thrive in the most arid situations. Half of the known species live in South Africa, while the others seek the warm temperate regions of the rest of the world. Some are in the habit of forming little rosettes around the main one and are called "hen-and-chickens" in consequence. They are adapted to planting in rockeries and edgings and are a familiar sight in conservatories and home gardens. Judged by popular favor, no rockery is complete without some representative of this group, such as the live-forever, sedum, house-leek or bryophyllum.

LIVE-FOREVER

COTYLEDON PULVERULENTA

(Plate 20, fig. 1)

Where there is sufficient moisture, the live-forevers may reach a height of five feet, with slender inflorescences of crimson and yellow that radiate from the stem like bright streamers. On exposed and arid hillsides of southern California the plants become dwarfed and the fleshy leaves at the base of the stem are less conspicuously covered with the white powder usually found there in this species.

The curving of the leaves where they clasp the stem has suggested the name cotyledon, which means cavity, while their succulence, which enables the plants to withstand severe drouth, has given rise to the term live-forever.

SAXIFRAGE FAMILY

SAXIFRAGACEÆ

Saxifrages prefer the coolness of alpine heights, having originally come from the mountains of Europe and the northern parts of the world. Some are found on old walls and rocks or in shady groves, but there are none at all in the tropics.

The members of this family have taken one step of advance over the roses in the joining of the separate pistils into one ovary, and all stages of the union are represented in the range of species. The gooseberries and currants are considered here as belonging to the family, although kept separate in some manuals. They are especially valued for their fruits, but there are some also that are unusually ornamental. Many of the true saxifrages are placed with their near relatives, the stonecrops, in rock and alpine gardens, but they are less well-known than other members of the group, such as the hydrangea, mock-orange, syringa and coral-bells.

PLATE 20

STONECROP FAMILY

SAXIFRAGE FAMILY

FIREWEED FAMILY

6
3
4
2
5
1

YELLOW SAXIFRAGE

Saxifraga hirculus

(Plate 20, fig. 2)

The slender stem of this yellow saxifrage seems scarcely sufficient to bear the golden cup of a flower at the end. It is an inconspicuous little perennial that blooms unobtrusively all summer long in subalpine or arctic bogs, where it is cold and damp.

The name saxifrage means rock-breaker and refers to the habit many of these plants have of sending their roots into crevices in the rocks, thus aiding in their disintegration by means of the carbon dioxid which is given off during growth. This result was thought by the ancients to indicate that the plants were able to dissolve stones in the bladder and they were accordingly prescribed for this ailment.

GARNET GOOSEBERRY

Ribes speciosum

(Plate 20, fig. 3)

The long curving branches of the garnet gooseberry, thickly set with dark shining leaves and hung with crimson blossoms like pendant jewels, lend a touch of Christmas gaiety to the canyons of southern California, for their effect is very like that of holly wreaths and berries in a setting of spring verdure instead of snow and evergreens. The brilliantly colored blossoms hang down on the underside of the branches, and their long crimson stamens form a fine fringe beaded at the tips with blue-green or yellow anthers. A tiny black bee may alight on these and pack the pollen into its pollen-baskets, then climbing the slender filaments as a small boy does a pole, suck the nectar from the base of the corolla-tube until, satisfied, it flies away. Or, with a hum like that of a giant bumble-bee, a swift dart on rapid wings, a flash of iridescent crimson and green, the humming-bird has come and gone, having sucked the nectar from a dozen blossoms with incredible swiftness.

The garnet gooseberry is not entirely dependent upon its winged friends. As the bud opens, the style is protruding and the anthers are visible at the edge of the corolla-tube. The stamen filaments slowly lengthen until the anthers cluster about the stigma upon which they shed their pollen in quick succession. When the pollen is all shed, the corolla withers, the filaments shrivel and twist and finally bring the mass of anthers and the style in contact. As the withered corolla falls, the green berry, covered with sticky red hairs, enlarges and turns red as it ripens. It then looks tempting enough to eat, but will be found quite inedible.

FLOWERING CURRANT

Ribes sanguineum malvaceum

(Plate 20, fig. 4)

The delicate pink of the hanging flower-clusters, combined with wrinkled leaves in soft tones of green, entitle the flowering currant to consideration as a decorative shrub, whether cultivated in gardens or growing wild in central and southern California. The species itself has redder blossoms than the variety illustrated and dark-purple berries that are rough-hairy, dry and bitter. The shrubs are tall and possess a fragrant resinous odor reminiscent of incense. They are to be found in the coast mountains as far north as British Columbia and southwards through California and Mexico and are hardy enough to be grown satisfactorily in eastern gardens.

GOLDEN CURRANT

Ribes aureum

(Plate 20, fig. 5)

Whiffs of a spicy fragrance announce the presence of the golden currant even before the long-tubed yellow blossoms are seen among the thin, light-green leaves of the shrubs. To an Easterner finding the blossoms in moist canyons on the coast, the golden currant conjures up memories of old-fashioned gardens at home, while the Middle-Westerner recognizes it as a wild-flower of hills and river-banks. Occasionally the tiny petals at the mouth of the pale-yellow tube are a bright red, and the berries may be either red or black as well as yellow. They have a sharply acid flavor that was appreciated by the Klamath Indians and causes them to be eagerly sought by others for pies, home-made jams and jellies.

FIREWEED FAMILY

ŒNOTHERACEÆ

The fireweeds constitute a distinct group which are regarded here as belonging on a branch line between the myrtles and cacti. It is also called the evening-primrose family from the many species that open in the evening and close in the morning. Many others, however, open and close in reverse order, and none of them are primroses structurally. The only point in common between the primroses proper and the evening-primroses is the primrose-yellow color of some species, so the preference is given here to the name of fireweeds. These are species that spring up in especial abundance after fire has swept the ground clear of vegetation.

Superficially the flowers of the fireweeds and especially of the yellow ones resemble those of the mustard because of the four-square arrangement of the petals. A decisive difference, however, is to be found in the position of the corolla on top of the ovary and in the eight stamens.

Besides the sweet and edible roots produced by several species of the group, they are mainly ornamental, not only as a large number of charming wild-flowers, but under cultivation, where may be found the vermilion-flowered zauschneria, the beautiful magenta blossoms of epilobium, showy clarkias and godetias, gay lopezias and a long list of œnotheras—white, pink or yellow.

HUMMING-BIRD TRUMPET

Zauschneria californica

(Plate 20, fig. 6)

In California the carnival of flowers reaches its height in spring when all vegetation has taken advantage of the winter rains. Hardier plants, which require less water or possess roots that are able to penetrate farther into the earth, constitute the lesser glory of the dry summer. In autumn when hills are sere and brown and only mountain retreats, brook-banks and bogs are fresh and flowery, shrubby plants or deep-rooted perennials may carry on the succession of bloom until a new season is ushered in by renewed rainfall. The humming-bird trumpet is a late loiterer that sets the dry or rocky hills of central and southern California ablaze with scarlet-vermilion blossoms. Their trumpet-shape and red color mark them as humming-bird flowers and suggest a name which is more suitable than that of California fuchsia, often used. The brilliant blossoms, set among attractive gray-green foliage, make this species desirable for masses of autumn bloom in the garden. The plants are perennial and easily grown from root-stocks.

There is another humming-bird trumpet (Zauschneria latifolia) which is even more striking because of its bright color. Both flowers and leaves are larger and the plants erect and bushy. They blossom also in the fall, but higher up in the mountains and rocky canyons of California, and will thrive equally well under cultivation.

FIREWEED

Epilobium angustifolium

(Plate 21, fig. 1)

Among the first to take advantage of ground laid bare by logging or fire in forests of spruce and fir, the narrow-leaved plants of the fireweed put forth long spires of rose-purple blossoms and turn scenes of desolation into gardens of beauty. In the autumn when the bright flowers have given place to purplish pods, the leaves take on the tints of the flames that earlier swept the ground and prepared the way. Although especially adapted to this work of reclamation, when there is none to be done the fireweed is content to decorate meadows and stream-banks, east, west, north and south at home, or abroad in Europe and Asia. So experienced a world traveler must perforce have developed some efficient method of getting about from place to place. The fluffy bunches of silky hairs, which burst from the ripened pods and float away on the faintest breeze, furnish the solution, even though the seed attached to each tuft of down is so tiny as to be difficult to see with the unaided eye.

From sunrise to sunset all summer long, a patch of fireweed is the scene of continuous movement and activity. Slowly, each in turn, the buds move upward from a hanging position to a horizontal one, folding back the four narrow reddish sepals, then the gay petals which often take a four-square position like the wings of a butterfly. Now bumble-bees and honey-bees add their swift motion to the picture—alighting on the flowers, probing for nectar, collecting the pollen and packing it into compact masses on their hind-legs—buzzing and humming the while. Meanwhile the stamens and style rise and droop, bend and twist, performing their appointed tasks with wonderful precision and such effectiveness that when their work is done, each flower is replaced by a long crimson pod. Within this are the tiny seeds attached to silken parachutes, ready when the pod bursts, to sail away and start anew the round of life.

The normally slender wand-like plants of the fireweed become stocky and branching under cultivation, each branch ending in a spire of flowers which bloom in quick succession and produce unusual and striking mass-effects. The young shoots are eaten as a pot-herb in Sweden, while in Russia the leaves are employed largely for making a beverage, and both roots and leaves have been used in medicine at different times and in different ways.

The name epilobium is derived from Greek words meaning upon the pod, and refers to the position of the corolla at the top of the ovary.

GODETIA

Godetia quadrivulnera

(Plate 21, fig. 2)

The charm of this small-flowered godetia may suffer by comparison with its more gorgeous sisters, but taken alone, the rich purple cups borne on slender stems possess a beauty not to be

Plate 21

FIREWEED FAMILY

1
2
3
4
5
6

denied as they respond to the call of spring on dry hillsides and in open places of the chaparral. They are also to be found among the pines at lower altitudes, but never very far north.

FAREWELL-TO-SPRING

GODETIA AMŒNA

(Plate 21, fig. 3)

The larger godetias are among the most charming of spring flowers and several resemble each other so closely as to be difficult to distinguish. The blossoms are large and cupped, the petals of a delicate satiny texture and the ground-color pinkish-lavender to rose-purple, often variegated with spots and markings of fiery rose-red. The species illustrated is so esteemed as to be cultivated abroad, while Dame Nature takes care of it in America, all along the western coast. The flowers are usually crimson, blotched with a deeper shade, but white ones occur occasionally, and in the garden double blossoms sometimes appear.

Mountain meadows, from central California to Oregon, are the localities in which a similar species (Godetia viminea) may be found; this has crimson petals that are paler towards the base and blotched with purple. In southern California as far as the Mexican border, another lovely godetia (Godetia bottæ) decorates hillsides near the coast with lilac flowers marked with purple.

The name farewell-to-spring refers to the fact that although they begin to bloom early in the season, many of them continue to blossom up to the very end, their gay colors waving a farewell after grasses and other herbs have turned brown and dry.

FRINGED CLARKIA

CLARKIA CONCINNA

(Plate 21, fig. 4)

Bright patches of rose-purple on shady slopes in the coast mountains of California betray the presence of the fringed clarkia, while a nearer view reveals the oddity of the individual blossoms. Instead of a prim regularity they present an almost fantastic appearance, with flaring petals cut into ribbons and raying out from narrow bases. Another clarkia (Clarkia pulchella), sometimes called pink fairies, is very similar but confines itself to the mountain slopes of Oregon and Washington and eastward to the Rockies.

These flowers are named in honor of Captain William Clark of the Lewis and Clark expedition that crossed the American continent in 1804-6 and found time in the midst of many arduous undertakings, to collect the plants of a new world.

TALL CLARKIA

CLARKIA ELEGANS

(Plate 21, fig. 5)

The rose-purple blossoms of this clarkia show their resemblance to their cousins the true fireweeds, in both shape and color of the four-square blossoms. The stems often grow to a height of six feet and the flowers are borne towards the ends of the branches, intermingled with leaves. They are quite common in spring and early summer in the chaparral belt of central and southern California, where they often form lovely masses of color on hillside and lower mountain-slope.

Clarkias are hardy annuals which respond readily to cultivation in a warm light soil, either partly shaded or fully exposed, and they will sometimes produce double forms or white varieties. They are especially pleasing when planted in grassy places, for they continue to bloom long after the grasses have turned yellow, and furnish a most effective background for the richly colored blossoms. The cut flowers will keep fresh for a week or more and the buds continue to open for some time.

SUN-CUPS

ŒNOTHERA BISTORTA

(Plate 21, fig. 6)

The leafy stems of the sun-cups, thickly set with bright golden disks, trail over the warm sands of the coast of southern California where the wind is cool and there is plenty of moisture, or they lift themselves more stiffly erect on plain and hill, where herb and grass also seek a share of light and water. A dark-brown spot at the base of each petal emphasizes the clear yellow which turns a rich orange-red as the flower fades. A reddish tinge on stems and seed-pods and the gray-green of the leaves add still greater variety of coloring to the whole.

Although belonging to what is usually called the evening-primrose family, sun-cups is a day-bloomer, as is indicated by this name. There is, however, some disagreement as to the origin of the term œnothera, but it seems to have had some connection with the drinking of wine. The roots of the common evening-primrose (Œnothera biennis) were used to scent the beverage or to arouse an appetite for it. They are sweet and edible, and have long been eaten as a table vegetable before the introduction of the potato into general use.

The yellow evening-primrose (Œnothera missouriensis) of the middle western plains bears magnificent blossoms which are sometimes as large as six or eight inches in diameter, while an almost equally large white-flowered species (Œnothera cæspitosa) ventures further west across the Colorado plains and up into the lower parts of the Rockies. This beautiful blossom opens between five and seven o'clock in the evening, the delicate white petals folding back and smoothing out their crinkles in from two to seven minutes, so that the movement, usually imperceptibly slow in other flowers, may easily be seen. The whiteness of the fully opened flowers is so conspicuous even in the dark, that night-flying hawk-moths have no trouble in finding them, and the four-inch tube of the blossom, more than half-full of nectar, is sufficient reward for night-work. The moths dart about from flower to flower, poising in the air over each fragrant blossom as they unroll tongues long enough to reach to the bottom of even the longest tube, and sipping until the supply is exhausted. They continue to visit the flowers until an hour or so after dark, or even longer if the nectar holds out. The next morning sees the fresh white blossoms of the evening before, drooping and wilted, but turned such a lovely pink as to still be attractive.

The common evening-primrose (Œnothera biennis), which

may be found generally in waste places, is also a favorite with hawk-moths. It too opens at dusk and so quickly that the movement is plainly evident. Since moths are not always at hand to bring about cross-pollination, an efficient method of self-pollination has been effected by many of the evening-primroses. The stigma emerges from the bud just before this is ready to open, and its four lobes soon spread out into a cross that may be easily dusted with pollen by insect-visitors. When the flower opens, the style bends to one side out of the way of the pollen from ripening anthers, but as the corolla wilts, the petals close together, bringing both anthers and stigma into close contact so that the latter receives home-grown pollen as a last resort.

Many species of evening-primroses are already under cultivation and they are well worth attention for the ease with which they may be grown and the wealth of beautiful flowers that are produced.

LOASA FAMILY

Loasaceæ

This comparatively small family is rather an odd group characterized particularly by stinging or barbed hairs and a flower structure similar to that of the cacti, with many sepals, petals and stamens, all on the top of the ovary. They are all except one genus South American, with a few in western North America. A few are already under cultivation and a number of wild species are beautiful enough to be introduced into gardens also.

MORNING-STAR

Mentzelia aurea

(Plate 22, fig. 1)

The morning-stars bear large five-pointed canary-yellow blossoms, with a satiny sheen to the petals, a glowing orange-red center and a feathery mass of stamens. They open early in the morning, when their fragrance attracts what bees may be abroad at the time. They may be companioned in their native haunts, which are stony streamways in the California mountains, by the blazing-star (Mentzelia levicaulis) which responds to the touch of sunlight by spreading glossy petals into a five or ten-pointed star. These flowers are unusually large, from three to five inches in diameter, and are borne in clusters on stout branching plants with shining white stems which grow also in the Great Basin as well as in the interior valleys and canyons of California.

In the late afternoon or early evening, when the morning-stars are folding their petals and going to sleep, bumble-bees and honey-bees begin to look about for fresh supplies of nectar and may then be seen alighting on the buds of the evening-star (Mentzelia multiflora) or hovering about waiting for them to open. At about four o'clock in the afternoon the ten bright yellow petals fold back and reveal a feathery group of stamens, whereupon visitors arrive in fairly large numbers to take their toll of both pollen and nectar. As the sun goes down the crowd grows less, but some of the more diligent work away until dark. This evening-star is a lover of the plains and lower mountains of the South and West and its flowers are smaller and yellower than are those of the species (Mentzelia ornata) of the Great Plains, with fragrant, cream-colored blossoms.

NOON-FLOWER FAMILY

Mesembryanthemaceæ

This small family with the long name is very close to the cactus group, which it resembles in the many petals and stamens placed at the top of the ovary, but the latter has many cells instead of one as in the cacti, and the leaves are normal. Noon-flowers are mainly South African, though a few are found in the Mediterranean region, Australia and America. Many seem to find favor as food with the inhabitants of the countries they occupy; the Australians pickle the leaves of a species they call pig's-face, while the seeds of the Shama are considered an important part of the diet of the desert Arabs. The people on the borders of the great African Desert use the leaves of still another species as a vegetable, and the seeds are ground into a sort of flour. Soda, narcotics and various drugs are obtained from still others, and along the Pacific Coast two species are grown as ornamentals.

Plate 22

LOASA FAMILY

NOON-FLOWER FAMILY

CACTUS FAMILY

BUCKTHORN FAMILY

PARSLEY FAMILY

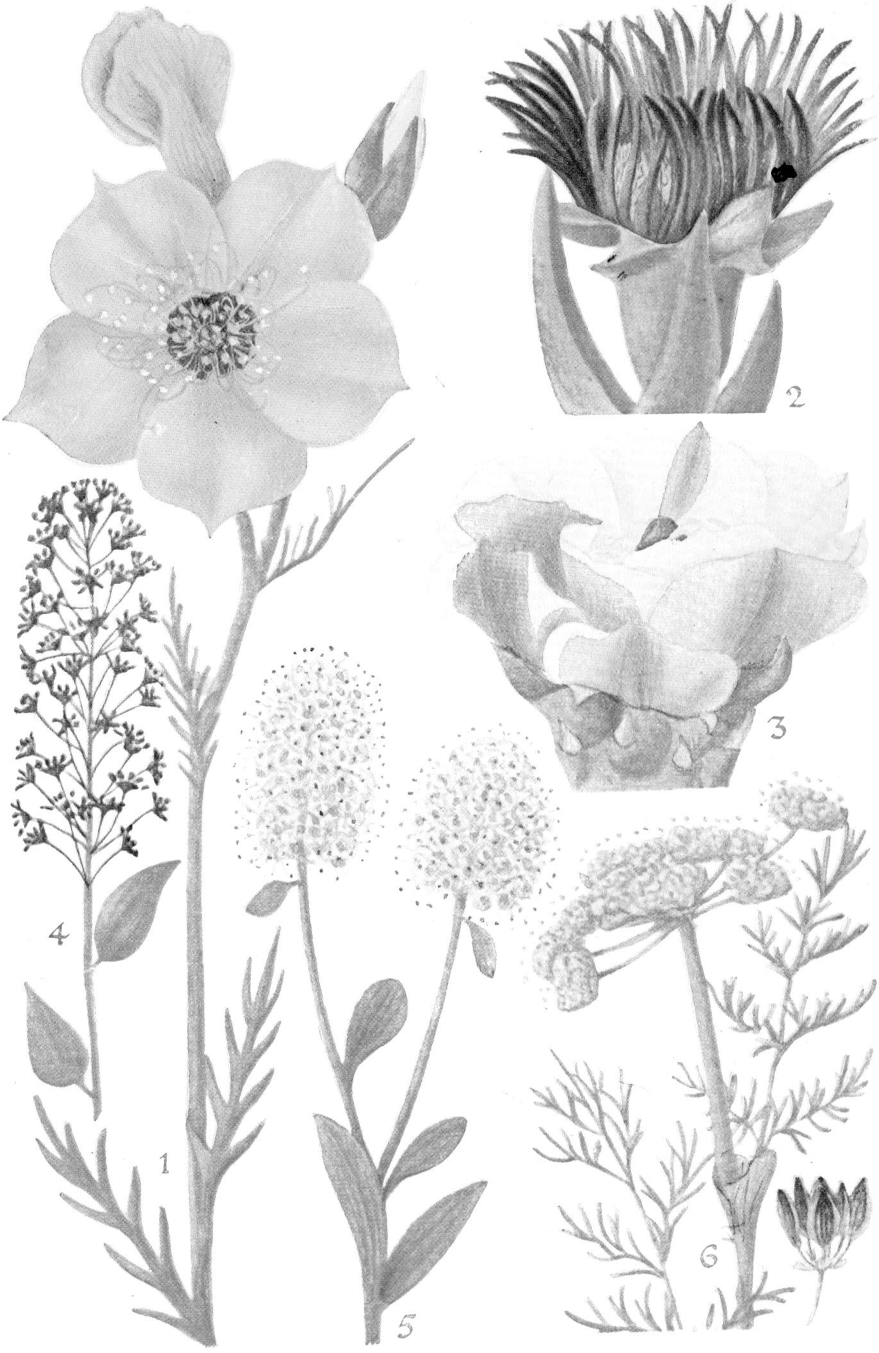
1
2
3
4
5
6

NOON-FLOWER

Mesembryanthemum æquilaterale

(Plate 22, fig. 2)

Along the sea-coast from San Francisco to Patagonia, the trailing juicy stems and leaves of the noon-flower hang curtains of vivid green over the cliffs or spread soft mats on the bare earth. An early morning or late afternoon sight of this verdure gives no hint of the transformation to be wrought by a bright noon-day, but under the caressing touch of the sun's rays, scores of bright magenta petals curve outward and form a thick fringe about the mass of pale yellow stamens in the center. There are hundreds of these blossoms, which are three or four inches in diameter and fragrant, but in the shadow or at evening the petals fold together again, shutting up shop until another sunny day.

The long scientific name means mid-day flower, and is only approximately descriptive, since the blossoms open when the air reaches a certain temperature, whether at ten o'clock or at noon. This species, which is distinguished by three-sided leaves, has been brought into this country from its home in Africa. The fruits are said to be palatable, and since they somewhat resemble small figs, the plants are sometimes called fig-marigold or sea-fig.

The ice-plant (Mesembryanthemum crystallinum) has been introduced into California and grows on the mesas and cliffs of the southern coast, where it flowers in the spring. The foliage is covered with shining drops of a gummy substance, which glistens in the sunshine like frost or ice, and the small cream-colored or pale-pink blossoms produce brown fruits that will open into five-pointed stars when placed in water, and reveal the tiny black seeds within. They will repeat this performance a number of times if permitted to become dry beforehand.

CACTUS FAMILY

Cactaceæ

The cacti are all American, and the great arid regions of Mexico and our own Southwest attract travelers from far and wide by the variety and oddity of form, and beauty of blossom exhibited by these strange plants. In response to the long periods of drouth to which they are exposed, they have dispensed with all leaves and have enlarged their stems and branches into great storage reservoirs. These may take the form of huge barrel-like structures such as those of the bisnaga, the pulp of which is often pounded and mashed by the Mexicans or travelers in the desert, until enough water is extracted to quench thirst; or immense tree-like trunks, towering thirty or forty feet high, with a few fantastically curving branches, such as the giant cactus. Others have many slender parallel erect trunks, as the organ cactus, while the spiny chollas look like bristling Teddy-bears, and the prickly pears cover vast areas with flat leaf-like joints that form impenetrable thickets in some localities. Many of the cacti have edible fruits and all have beautiful blossoms, with numerous silken petals and golden centers of hundreds of stamens. As the colors range from white through pale lemon-yellow to brilliant crimson and magenta, a desert with the cacti in full bloom possesses all the exotic charm of a scene from the Arabian Nights.

YELLOW PRICKLY-PEAR

OPUNTIA ENGELMANNI

(Plate 22, fig. 3)

The yellow prickly-pear bears large flowers, several inches across, made up of many lemon-colored petals which are tinged with red and of a silken transparency, and a central mass of golden stamens. The fruits may be found on the market in California, for they are sweet and edible, with a red pulp, but care must be taken to avoid the barbs. The American Indians had long been cultivating various species of the prickly-pears when America was discovered, and at that time explorers took them to Spain and its colonies whence they have spread to all warm countries. The fruits are highly nutritious and form a large part of the food of the Arabs of Northern Africa, where they are cultivated extensively for home consumption. The natives of Sicily grow such a fine quality of fruit that it is exported to New York and other American cities.

The yellow prickly-pear is also a honey producer, especially in Texas, where it is unusually abundant. The honey is light amber in color, somewhat granular and with a strong flavor. The flat stems of the plants are also useful in furnishing forage for cattle during periods of drouth when other feed is scarce or lacking. The stock do not eat the spiny opuntias from choice, but when forced to do so or starve, they may escape starvation only to die from the effects of the masses of sharp spines on the alimentary tract.

BUCKTHORN FAMILY

Rhamnaceæ

The buckthorn family to which the ornamental blueblossoms belong are useful to man in furnishing drugs, fruits, dyes and honey. The well-known tonic-laxative, cascara sagrada or sacred bark, is obtained from a buckthorn of the Northwest, while frangula, a still more powerful drug of the same sort, is derived from a species that is native to Europe but occasionally grows wild in the East. This also furnishes woollen dyes, the bark producing a yellow and the ripe berries blues and greens. The jujube tree of the African shore of the Mediterranean bears a pulpy fruit that was celebrated among the ancients and is still eaten, while other species of the same group furnish similarly edible fruits.

CEANOTHUS

Ceanothus cyaneus

(Plate 22, fig. 4)

There are many different species of ceanothus in the Pacific Coast region, all extremely attractive shrubs with shiny leaves and feathery clusters of tiny blossoms ranging in color from pure white, through azure blue, to the dark purple-blue of the variety illustrated, which occurs locally in San Diego county only. The deerbrush (Ceanothus integerrimus), with showy clusters of white or pale blue flowers, is a favorite of the deer, which enjoy eating the soft leaves, flexible branches and bark flavored like wintergreen. This grows in the mountains, from southern California to Oregon, and in the Yosemite. The red-root or New Jersey tea (Ceanothus americanus) of the East also has white flowers and leaves that were used for tea during the Revolutionary War. The roots are red and astringent with a high percent of tannin, and the flowers so fragrant that they are visited by a very large number of different kinds of insects. Both pollen and honey are yielded by the creamy white, fragrant blossoms of the snow-bush (Ceanothus velutinus) which is distributed over the coast ranges of California and to the north and east.

BLUEBLOSSOM

Ceanothus thyrsiflorus

(Plate 22, fig. 5)

Of the many floral harbingers of spring, none is lovelier than this species of Ceanothus, as the plumy clusters of azure flowers burst into bloom over chaparral covered hillsides or among the redwood trees. The shrubs are shiny-leaved and evergreen, and the blossoms fragrant. If rubbed up with water, the latter will form an interesting lather that is a satisfactory substitute for soap, but they will cause disappointment if gathered for bouquets, for the tiny flowers fade rapidly and drop off soon after being picked.

PARSLEY FAMILY

Apiaceæ (Umbelliferae)

Physician, confectioner and housewife daily accept the services of the great family to which the familiar parsley gives its name. Avoiding all localities in the tropics except the mountains, these "umbrella-bearers" are at hand in other parts of the world, ready to supply timely aid in case of need. The old family name is a fanciful reference to the arrangement of the tiny flowers in flat-topped spreading clusters and not to any need of protection against rain.

Apart from this distinctive arrangement of the blossoms, the members of the group may often be distinguished by a peculiar and indescribable odor that is usually detected in the fruit and sometimes pervades the entire plant. This is due to a volatile oil stored in tiny reservoirs and is the basis of some medicines, liqueurs and confectionery.

It is a far cry from the fœtid, repellent odors of asafœtida and coriander to the spicy aromas of anise, sweet-cicely, caraway and myrrh, but one and all spring from a common stock. Likewise there lurks the difference of life and death between the parsley and the fool's-parsley, the water-parsnip and the water-hemlock, the edible celery and carrot and the poison-hemlock; between the vegetable parsnip so nutritious when cultivated in the garden and the same parsnip, so deadly when growing wild.

Of the many different families of flowers, the umbellifers are the most popular with insects as a whole, and although they are not particularly good honey-plants nor favorites with the bees, there are hosts of other fliers, creepers and crawlers that swarm about continually in search of pollen and nectar. Over two hundred different sorts of visitors have been collected from several species of this family.

There are comparatively few ornamentals in the group, but of these, the blue lace-flower and several varieties of sea-holly are admired for their showy heads of blue blossoms.

WILD PARSLEY

PEUCEDANUM UTRICULATUM

(Plate 22, fig. 6)

The feathery foliage and yellow flower clusters of the wild parsley are familiar sights on the mesas and grassy foothills of southern California in early spring. Later in the season broad-winged fruits, which resemble brown-striped bugs, take the place of the blossoms.

The sanicle (Sanicula menziesi) looks very much like the wild parsley, but has less finely cut leaves and prefers moist woods and clay soils in the same region. In late summer or autumn the absence of other blossoms in the landscape enhances the delicate beauty of the fennel (Fœniculum vulgare), as the tall graceful plants, with spreading stems and finely cut gray-green foliage, line roadsides or spread a mist of yellow over waste fields. The flowers and crushed herbage give forth a spicy fragrance like that of anise (Pimpinella anisum) and for which it is often cultivated.

Marshy places along the coast are made beautiful in the spring by the stems and plumy foliage of the water-hemlock (Cicuta occidentalis), which bears white parsley-like blossoms. It is poisonous like its eastern relative (Cicuta maculata), which is one of the commonest swamp or brookside plants and one of the most deadly. The root tastes good and has been known to cause the deaths of children and of hungry hikers who find the attractive-looking roots by chance and are ignorant of their nature. Occasionally poisoning has occurred from drinking water in which the roots have been bruised by trampling. Socrates' death was caused by a drink made from a very similar plant, the poison-hemlock (Conium maculatum), also common along waysides and a source of danger to children who like to make whistles from the hollow stems, or to their elders who mistake the roots for parsnips. While the poison-hemlock was popular among the ancients as a method of executing criminals and was widely used as a medicinal drug, modern research has limited its use to that of a narcotic, especially for calming maniacal excitement.

The nectar of the parsleys is fully exposed and the process by which self-fertilization is avoided is clearly illustrated by the flowers of the huge cow-parsnip (Heracleum lanatum), the coarse hairy plants of which bear immense umbrella-like clusters of white blossoms and are a familiar sight in moist situations at moderate altitudes. There are five stamens, but when the bud opens only one is visible, the other four being compactly curled up under the curving petals. As the flower matures, the filaments uncurl and lengthen, one after another, carrying the anther up where the pollen is accessible to insects but at some distance from the stigma. The latter remains immature until all the stamen filaments have turned downward beneath its level and all the pollen has been shed. Then the style branches lengthen somewhat and the stigmatic surface becomes receptive to pollen. If none is brought from other flowers by insect visitors, no seeds are produced and this species is in consequence entirely dependent upon its insect friends.

HONEYSUCKLE FAMILY

CAPRIFOLIACEÆ

The honeysuckles are mostly woody plants that are cultivated in Europe for the drugs to be obtained from them, while many of the climbers are favorites in this country for their beauty and fragrance. The coralberry, snowberry and elderberry possess ornamental fruits, and those of the common elderberry in the East, which are black with a red juice, are valued for making pies and flavoring wine. The fragrant flowers occur in large cream-colored flat-topped inflorescences and are under suspicion of being poisonous when fresh, but are used by the pharmacist when dried. They are also utilized to give a Muscat flavor to certain wines abroad. The mountain elder produces brilliant red berries from cream-colored blossoms, while the blue elderberry of California and Oregon has beautiful clusters of large blackish fruits with a blue "bloom." Both are said to be employed as food by the Indians, and the latter species is reported as an important source of pollen but not of nectar. Of the viburnums, the best known in the garden is the variety called snowball, with large globe-like masses of white flowers, while of the honeysuckles proper there are a large number of fragrant and beautiful varieties. The fruits of some of the bush species are used as emetics or cathartics and those of the common honeysuckle are made into a syrup which was formerly recommended for asthma. The fragrant blossoms of the latter also yield a perfume.

PINK HONEYSUCKLE

LONICERA HISPIDULA

(Plate 23, fig. 1)

This honeysuckle of the western coast lacks the fragrance of its better known relatives of the garden, but the delicately pink

Plate 23

HONEYSUCKLE FAMILY

BLUEBELL FAMILY

5
6
7
2
1
3
4

blossoms are very similar in form. It is also something of a climber and is usually found clambering over trees and shrubs in the canyons and along streams, from British Columbia to California.

The trumpet honeysuckle (Lonicera sempervirens) is one of the garden favorites throughout the country, growing wild east of the Rockies. It is a vigorous climber and although it lacks fragrance, attracts humming-birds by its bright red coloring and abundant nectar. The other garden favorite (Lonicera periclymenum) opens pale blossoms at dusk and sends forth such a powerful perfume that hawk-moths perceive it from a distance of three hundred yards and fly, straight as an arrow, to the nectar glands.

BLACK TWINBERRY

Lonicera involucrata

(Plate 23, fig. 2)

The orange-red or yellow blossoms of the black twinberry appear here and there in pairs along the tall woody stems. These plants show a preference for moist places among the hills and mountains of the Sierra Nevada and coast ranges, or in the woodlands north to British Columbia. Beneath each pair of twin blossoms are two broad leafy bracts that turn bright crimson as the flowers fade, and turning back, finally reveal two shining black berries that look delicious but are bitter to the taste.

The fly honeysuckle (Lonicera ciliata) of northern woodlands bears two pendulous yellowish-green flowers, with nectar so attractive to bumble-bees that they frequently cut the buds into shreds in their haste to reach it. Many of the honeysuckles have tubes suitable only for humming-birds and hawk-moths and far too long and narrow for honey-bees. The corolla of the black twinberry, however, is well adapted to the short tongues of the latter and they are able to furnish a surplus of honey near the coast of British Columbia, where the flowers are especially abundant.

TWINFLOWER

Linnæa borealis

(Plate 23, fig. 3)

Twice charmed are the northern woods whose cool shadows are brightened by the fairy-like grace of the twinflower, since the shining mats of evergreen leaves carpeting the forest floor are scarcely less attractive than the fragrant pink blossoms nodding above. They are especially abundant in Sweden and were especial favorites of the great botanist of that country, Linnæus, after whom they were named.

The blossom keeps its nectar stowed away at the base of the corolla, protected against rain by the inverted position and guarded against the depredations of small unwelcome flies by many interwoven hairs in the throat. It seems to have no attraction for bumble-bees, which disdain to even stop and look as they buzz noisily by. Only the dance-fly is invited to pause in its light-winged dartings to and fro, up and down, and take a sip or to cease the airy blowing of bubbles for the delight of its lady-love long enough to carry the pollen from flower to flower.

Not only do northern woods in this country, Europe and Asia offer a home to this little evergreen plant, but wherever there is moisture and coolness—in the bogs of New England, northwards in the Rockies and Sierra Nevada from California northwest to the Alaskan Islands—there it also may be found, creeping over the ground and perfuming the air. It will also thrive under cultivation if given a porous soil of mold or peat, especially if shaded.

SNOWBERRY

Symphoricarpus racemosus

(Plate 23, fig. 4)

Coralberry and snowberry—red berry and white—cling to the bushes from late summer through the autumn days and well into winter, often adding their pearly lustre and cheery red to many a wintry landscape. In the spring, after the snow has melted from rocky banks in the northern states and the rains have soaked into the California hills, the snowberry puts forth a wealth of smooth green leaves and as the season advances conceals among them drooping clusters of pale-pink bell-flowers. Honey-bees early seek them out and often glean enough honey to be of importance to the bee-keeper of the West, especially in Washington and British Columbia. The inconspicuous white or pink blossoms of the snowberry (Symphoricarpus occidentalis) and the coralberry (Symphoricarpus vulgaris) of the East render a similar service, and the berries of the latter also serve to succor many a small bird when the ground is covered with snow.

The Greek term symphoricarpos refers to the occurrence of the berries in thick clusters. Although not often found under cultivation, these low smooth-leaved shrubs, with their slender branches bending under a weight of beautiful red or white berries, are excellent for planting in massed groups or for covering the ground under trees. They will thrive in almost any soil and are ornamental the year round.

BLUEBELL FAMILY

Campanulaceæ

The bluebells and lobelias are here placed in the same family since they are more alike than different in their main characteristics. The former has a milky juice in stem and leaves, combined with a sweet mucilaginous substance that gives the roots of some species a certain food value. The juice of the lobelias, on the other hand, is very poisonous, blistering the skin when applied externally and producing serious or fatal inflammation internally. Children especially should be warned against Indian tobacco (Lobelia inflata), a common weed of roadside and field in the East, which tempts them by its familiar name to experiments in smoking.

Both bluebells and lobelias occur in many charming garden varieties, of which the huge clusters of many-colored Canterbury-bells, the scarlet cardinal flower and purple lobelia are the most favored.

BLUEBELL

Campanula rotundifolia

(Plate 23, fig. 5)

Unaware of world-wide, age-old fame in song and story, graceful bluebells nod on slender stems, from rocky banks or grassy mountain slopes in the northern hemisphere, the world round. If insect visitors fail to heed the invitation to carry pollen from flower to flower, the movements of anthers and stigma take place with precision and perform their appointed tasks unaided by bee or butterfly. Young buds start their careers proudly erect, but as they grow larger and heavier the thread-like pedicel bends under their weight slowly to a horizontal and finally to a drooping position. The anthers of the half-opened flower clasp the roughened surface of the style closely and as they burst, deposit grains of blue-green pollen thickly over the outside, causing it to look like a tiny fuzzy blue cat-tail. Having performed their work, the stamens shrink into diminutive curls at the bottom of the corolla, the stigma-lobes curve further and further until they come in contact with the pollen grains clinging to the outer surface of the style and so the transfer of pollen to stigma is brought about.

Campanula means little bell, but although the corollas are always bell-shaped, they exhibit considerable variation in size and outline, from short and broad with widely flaring lobes to long and narrow with straighter lines. One and all are some shade of blue-lavender and possess an airy grace that is lacking in the Canterbury-bell (Campanula medium) of the garden, with its larger flowers of heavier texture. White-flowered bluebells occur under cultivation and there is also an interesting variety (Campanula r. soldanellæflora) which has semi-double blue blossoms split to the base into about twenty-five ribbon-like segments. This is named after a little fringed blue primrose (Soldanella) of the Alps which interests travelers because of its habit of coming up through the snow.

DOWNINGIA

DOWNINGIA ELEGANS

(Plate 23, fig. 6)

Wherever found, the lavender-blue blossoms and soft green leaves of downingia turn unsightly muddy spots into miniature gardens of loveliness. They can easily be persuaded to transfer their beauty to garden or room if care is taken to carry a section of the mud in box or pan so that the roots are undisturbed.

Another downingia (Downingia pulchella) is similar but smaller in every way. It too grows in muddy spots in California and Oregon or ventures eastward to Nevada and Idaho.

CARDINAL-FLOWER

LOBELIA CARDINALIS

(Plate 23, fig. 7)

Most brilliant of all our red flowers and extremely showy against a background of the dark-green of leaves and the pale-green of grasses, the cardinal-flower may occasionally be found in wet places in the mountains. The leafy stems stretch up among swamp grasses to a height of several feet and bear one-sided spikes of intensely cardinal-red blossoms with slender tubes and long narrow lobes. Bees are unable to reach the nectar at the base of the tube, but ruby-throated humming-birds are not only more fortunate in this respect but catch a red signal more quickly than any other color.

Lobelia is named for L'Obel, a botanist of Flanders in the sixteenth century, while the species cardinalis and cardinal-flower both refer to the distinctive shade of red in the blossoms. The term for this color harks back to a Greek word for heart, which we find also in "cardiac," so that cardinal-red is a synonym for blood-red, the color that is worn by cardinals of the church and the cardinal-bird.

Swamps, ditch-banks and low wet ground in the eastern part of the country, south to Florida and west to the borders of Texas are the favored haunts of the cardinal-flower which has also invaded similar places in the mountains of southern California. It may be induced to spread more widely in the state, especially if lovers or makers of gardens take advantage of its willingness to thrive in any rich damp soil. Since it is a perennial and needs little care, it will richly repay cultivation.

The low-growing purple lobelia (Lobelia erinus) is already a familiar sight in many gardens and grows usually in borders, covered with a profusion of small flowers. There are numerous varieties of this species, some suitable for vases or baskets because of their graceful habit of growth; others with yellowish or bronze foliage and still others which produce white, rose, blue or crimson blossoms, so that a lobelia garden does not lack for variety. A large-flowered lobelia (Lobelia syphilitica) is a hardy perennial with blue or purplish blossoms. This also grows wild in wet places in the eastern half of the country and formerly enjoyed considerable repute in medical practice.

ASTER FAMILY

Asteraceæ

The aster family stands at the end of the central line of development from the buttercups through the roses. It frequently goes by the names of sunflower family and composite family also, the former because of a prominent genus and the latter on account of the arrangement of the separate flowers into a compact head. But no matter by what name this group of plants may be known, they stand for efficiency in the mechanism of the flower, for successful co-operation between the parts of the inflorescence, and for the production of offspring the best fitted to establish themselves in new homes and start sturdy families of their own.

The number and variety of this host are so great as to necessitate its being subdivided into tribes, each with its own traits and distinctive characteristics. The flowers range from the tiny insignificant ones of the ragweed with wind-borne pollen that is so obnoxious to hay-fever sufferers, through familiar daisy, aster, goldenrod and thistle of wayside and garden, to magnificent blooms of dahlia and chrysanthemum—the glory of flower shows and the pride of the horticulturalist. They furnish tonics and stimulants, food or forage, oils and dyes, beverages, medicines and poisons, and together with the grasses inherit the earth.

GOLDENROD

SOLIDAGO SEROTINA

(Plate 24, fig. 1)

Slim and rod-like or branched and feathery, goldenrods flare forth like yellow torches from marsh and river-bank, plain and hillside, in mountain meadow, roadside or field, until chill winds and soggy autumn days turn their glowing into brown ashes. All but three or four of the numerous species belong to North America and every condition of soil and climate the country over has its favorite sort. The one illustrated is especially fond of the North and West, from New Brunswick to British Columbia, but thrives also in the Southwest.

None but the specialist need be concerned with the difficult distinctions between the many kinds, although bee-keepers recognize wide differences in their value as honey-producers. The great variability in the abundance of nectar may be due to the environment, and while bees may be reaping a harvest of deep golden-yellow honey during an autumn in Maine, those of Iowa or California may pass the goldenrods entirely by.

Besides the honey-bees, there are a hundred or more other insects that bestow their attentions upon the goldenrods. The small green ground-beetles swarm over the florets in search of plant-lice and insect-eggs as well as pollen; the soldier-beetle may be found by the thousand sucking nectar, while other tiny beetles crawl into the cosy corners furnished by the close-set florets, to spend the night in air several degrees warmer than that outside.

With one exception all goldenrods are bright-yellow throughout, but in spite of this uniformity of color, honey-bees are remarkably clever in distinguishing between different species. If working on one with flat-topped clusters (Solidago graminifolia), they will pick it out unerringly, even when growing close to or even intermingled with another species that has flower heads in panicles

Plate 24

ASTER FAMILY

1
2
3
4
5
6

(Solidago rugosa). If interested in the cream-colored goldenrod (Solidago bicolor), they are not to be more than momentarily distracted by any other, even when clusters of these are placed directly in their path.

Solidago is derived from a Latin word meaning to make whole, in reference to the former use of these plants in the healing of wounds. The rod-like form of some of the species was considered by the Druids to indicate their use as divining rods for locating springs of fresh water or hidden treasures of gold and silver.

ASTER

Aster chilensis

(Plate 24, fig. 2)

Inseparable as Damon and Pythias, purple aster and yellow goldenrod appear side by side as signals to summer that her reign nears its close and autumn is at hand. Their appearance almost invariably together is a natural result of the immense number of different species of each and their occurrence among the fall flowers of nearly every state in the Union, but it has also been explained in a fanciful way. It is related that in the days of witches and fairies, a little golden-haired girl and one with starry blue eyes were inseparable companions in their play. Once upon a time, happening to be near a witch's hut during a rainstorm in the forest, they sought shelter beneath her roof, and marvelling at her power to change human beings into plants or various animals, requested to be transformed also. The wish of the girl with the golden hair was to become something that would make everyone who saw it, happy and cheerful, while her little friend asked nothing more than to be ever by her side. So it has come about that the starry blue eye of the aster is rarely far away from the bright yellow plume of the goldenrod.

Unlike goldenrods, the aster community of tiny yellow tube-flowers in the center of the head is surrounded by numerous long and narrow ray-flowers of contrasting color—pink, lavender, purple or white—that are more easily seen by bees at a distance and guide them more quickly to the supply of nectar. Although honey-bees have found that they save time and energy by visiting a single species of flower during the period of its blooming, they are just as unable to distinguish between the many species of aster as any but the experts are, and so visit them indiscriminately. Like the goldenrods, asters are erratic in their production of nectar, seeming to be similarly affected by changing conditions of soil and climate and more apt to produce an abundance where moisture is present than in dry localities.

As ornamentals, asters are easy of cultivation, and the wild varieties will doubtless improve much under garden conditions. The name of the aster is from the Greek word for star and refers to the star-like heads of flowers.

WOOLLY-ASTER

CORETHROGYNE FILAGINIFOLIA

(Plate 24, fig. 3)

The pink rays of the woolly-aster, encircling golden centers and borne on branches covered with soft white hairs, form a color-scheme that is unusually lovely against the dark-green of the chaparral. The leaves are small and clothed in a dense white wool which protects against the drying effect of late summer days rather than guards against the cold.

From southern California, all along the coast to Oregon, bare rocky ledges below an altitude of 5000 feet may offer a foothold to the woolly-aster, and although variations in leaf-shape and arrangement of the heads are frequent, the plants should be readily recognized by the characteristic combination of colors.

The odd name of the genus is derived from Greek words that refer to the brush-like tuft of hairs on the tips of the styles.

DAISY

ERIGERON DIVERGENS

(Plate 24, fig. 4)

The slender soft-hairy stems of this little daisy bear flower-heads with golden centers and violet or bright-pink rays, so like the aster as to be distinguished only by close inspection. The rays about the disk are generally found to be more numerous as well as narrower than those of an aster, although in some cases this distinction is by no means obvious.

The low tufts of gray-green foliage, combined with the gracefully borne flower heads, are charming wherever found—whether in the garden, the loose soil of the coast mountains or on plains and river banks eastward to Texas. There are many other species in the West, among which mention should be made of the mountain daisy (Erigeron salsuginosus), which is abundant in the higher mountains and in moist places from the far West to Colorado. This is a large handsome plant with heads an inch and a half across that are made up of yellow centers and lavender rays. The little alpine daisy (Erigeron uniflorus) takes root in the granite soil of the higher peaks and forms dense leafy mats with violet-rayed flowers on short stalks, while the seaside daisy (Erigeron glaucus) beautifies cliffs and sandy shores with large heads of flowers—yellow-centered and violet-rayed.

The Erigerons are American daisies, while the English daisy (Bellis perennis) is a little cousin from western Europe. This has been brought into American gardens, but "runs away" whenever it can and stars grassy lawns with dainty flower-heads, yellow-centered and with white or rose-colored rays. This is the daisy famed in history, legend and poetry. It was used frequently as an emblem on coats-of-arms in the days gone by and the flower itself seems to have been associated with many of the Queen Margarets of the past, probably because the French name for the daisy is marguerite. Margaret of Anjou chose it as her special flower and the blossoms became so associated with her that after her marriage to King Henry VI daisies were worn by all the nobles of the court and their wives and daughters when they welcomed her to England. The royal silver of that period also bears the emblem of the daisy engraved upon it. An Order of the Daisy was instituted in honor of Margaret of Flanders, while the sister of Frances I of France, the wife of King Humbert of Italy, and various other Margarets, were all associated with the flower in some way: floral offerings, engravings on signet rings or coats-of-arms, jewels of gold and pearls set as marguerites.

The name erigeron, applied to the American daisy, means early old and refers to the covering of white hairs on the outside of the buds, while daisy is a contraction of day's-eye in allusion to its cheery face in the sunshine and its going to sleep at night.

GUMWEED

Grindelia robusta

(Plate 24, fig. 5)

Ranged stiffly by the side of the road, the awkward yellow-headed gumweeds neither bend nor curtsy, and it is only the brisker breezes that can ruffle their dignity. The clumsy buds, with their narrow turned-back bracts, look like huge burs and are covered with a white gummy substance that makes them unpleasant to the touch. These resinous buds furnish a drug which was known to the Indians and used by them, as it was also by medical practitioners, for asthma and bronchitis, as well as for the eruptions caused by poison-ivy and poison-oak.

This species of gumweed is to be found in summer on dry hills in the western part of California. There are several other species along the coast which are quite similar in general appearance and recognizable as a rule by the resinous exudation. One of these (Grindelia cuneifolia) grows in salt marshes and on shores, flowering in October. It has a woody base to distinguish it from another shore-species (Grindelia glutinosa) which blooms somewhat earlier. On the plains and prairies, from the Mississippi River westward, the common species (Grindelia squarrosa) is often called rosin-weed and looks very much like the gumweed illustrated. This is much sought after by bees, but to the human palate the honey is inferior in flavor. Bee-keepers claim also that it candies too quickly to be desirable in the combs as a winter store and that the bees have to hurry home with their load to prevent its becoming candied in their sacks.

PENTACHÆTA

Pentachæta aurea

(Plate 24, fig. 6)

The bright golden disks of pentachæta, with their thick fringe of narrow rays, gleam among the grasses on a clear morning like miniature suns. They end the day's work in the afternoon when they fold the rays together and go to sleep, or they refuse to work at all if the temperature is too chill. They will do the same if gathered into a bouquet, and even though they may reluctantly open again, will retain a ragged, dejected appearance. Their spicy fragrance is something like that of goldenrod.

The plants thrive best in open ground even though somewhat dry, for in such spots they spread out into rosettes two feet across which are covered with bloom, while if crowded among the grasses and forced to compete for the means of existence, the stems grow singly to a few inches in length and bear but a few large heads. A scarcity of water in the soil may bring about under-nourishment to such an extent that the branches become thread-like, one or two inches tall, and the heads a quarter to half an inch across.

Only the southernmost counties of California seem to suit this stay-at-home, which strikes root in warm loose soil and blooms in the spring. Its name means five-bristles in reference to the sort of pappus possessed by the first-named species.

WYETHIA

Wyethia angustifolia

(Plate 25, fig. 1)

The great heads of wyethia, rich in tones of yellow, are veritable giants in the sunflower tribe. Each is borne on a stout stalk which rises from a resinous root and has at its base a group of large leaves with wavy margins. The localities favored by these plants are open plains and hills in the coast ranges and Sierra Nevada. It is said that the Hupa Indians enjoy eating the green shoots raw. Another species (Wyethia amplexicaulis), which is quite similar in appearance, occurs in moist valleys and plains,

Plate 25

ASTER FAMILY

1
2
3
4
5

from Colorado westward to Nevada and in the Rocky Mountains. It sometimes covers considerable areas with rich foliage and glowing flowers.

BUSH-SUNFLOWER

Encelia californica

(Plate 25, fig. 2)

The low dark-green shrubs of the bush-sunflower, covered with cheery brown and yellow flowers, are a conspicuous feature of the lower portion of the chaparral belt, where they brighten the landscape with bloom whatever the season. Although most at home on hills along the coast from Monterey to San Diego, they venture also as far east as Arizona. There and in the San Bernardino and Riverside Valleys, another species (Encelia farinosa) with gray leaves, covers the hills with silver and gold. This is sometimes called incense plant from its use in the churches of Lower California. The stems and branches are said to exude a resinous gum that is chewed by Indian children or made into a varnish by their elders, while the Mexicans warm it and use it in poultices.

The common sunflower (Helianthus annuus) of our western plains is perhaps the most famous of the bush-sunflower's relatives. Although execrated by the farmer of Kansas as a bothersome weed, it has been made his state flower, while among the Incas of Peru it was exalted to a high position in their ceremonies of sun-worship. In many countries it is cultivated for the sake of the seeds, which are used as food. The Jerusalem artichoke (Helianthus tuberosus) is a perennial sunflower that is valued for its sweet edible tubers.

COREOPSIS

Coreopsis tinctoria

(Plate 25, fig. 3)

The bright-yellow tips of the ray-flowers of coreopsis form golden halos about the rich crimson centers and enhance the airy grace of feathery foliage and slender flexible stems. The charming flower-heads bend and sway on these thread-like stalks and transform unsightly ditch-banks into scenes of loveliness. It is not a native of the coast, but has been brought in from the eastern part of the country and introduced into gardens. It is showy, easy to cultivate and deservedly popular as a consequence.

The Greek name is formed from words which describe the seed as resembling a bug or tick. There is also a common name, tickseed, which is frequently used.

DESERT COREOPSIS

COREOPSIS BIGELOVI

(Plate 25, fig. 4)

The pretty heads of the desert coreopsis in two shades of yellow—golden rays and orange centers—are borne on slender stems which spring from a tuft of shining, somewhat succulent and finely cut leaves. They brighten warm sandy places in southern California and nearby Arizona and are especially fond of the borders of the desert. A near relative (Coreopsis maritima), sometimes called sea-dahlia, on the contrary prefers the shore and forms one of the strikingly handsome plants of the coast of San Diego county and nearby islands. The succulent leaves, cut into narrow segments, are distinctive and unusually graceful, while the flower-heads with orange centers and bright-yellow rays are remarkably large and beautiful.

GOLDWEED

VERBESINA ENCELIOIDES

(Plate 25, fig. 5)

In spring and early summer the goldweed spreads a golden glory over fallow fields and waste places. The leafy branching plants grow to a height of several feet and bear many heads an inch or two in diameter. At home in Texas and southern Colorado to Arizona, it has traveled far and wide into the warmer parts of the country and may be found frequently also under cultivation.

TIDY-TIPS

Layia elegans

(Plate 26, fig.1)

The pure white edges of the scalloped rays of tidy-tips form pale halos around the golden centers and bestow an air of crisp freshness that is lacking in forms entirely yellow. Reddish purple stems and prettily cut leaves, silvered over with fine hairs, play their part in completing the beauty of the plants. They are quite worthy a prominent place in the garden and will repay cultivation with a wealth of bloom and luxuriant foliage.

Southern California possesses two species of tidy-tips which resemble each other so closely that it is necessary to pull the head apart and look carefully at its structure in order to determine which is which, even though the one (Layia platyglossa), which ranges farther north than Santa Barbara, is supposed to be less frequently pure yellow than the other (Layia elegans). Another lovely layia (Layia glandulosa), which has large heads with pure white rays about a yellow center, may be found in barren or sandy soil as far north as British Columbia and east to Idaho and New Mexico.

TARWEED

Hemizonia congesta lutescens

(Plate 26, fig. 2)

The tarweeds are not to be mistaken by one who tramps abroad in late summer or autumn, for the crushed herbage gives forth a distinctive spicy odor that is pleasant or disagreeable according to one's taste in perfumes. Leaves and stems are sticky with glandular hairs which make them unpleasant to handle and is the basis for the name tarweed. The genus is called hemizonia, which means half-girdle, because the bracts partly surround the seeds formed by the ray-flowers.

The tarweed illustrated is one of many forms of the species (Hemizonia congesta) which is white, as is also a tall variety (Hemizonia c., luzulæfolia), and both are found in hayfields. They usually grow in dry, open ground throughout California. Of the

Plate 26

ASTER FAMILY

5
4
1
2
3
6

twenty-five or more species in the state, three are sources of honey. The yellow tarweed (Hemizonia virgata), common in the valleys of the interior, yields large amounts during August. The honey is light yellow, with a good body and flavor. The coast tarweed (Hemizonia corymbosa) affords somewhat less, while the species (Hemizonia fasciculata), frequent south of San Francisco except on the desert, is an excellent producer, especially along the coast from Santa Barbara to San Diego. The honey is dark-amber in color, with a strong flavor, and is used largely in the manufacture of chewing tobacco and shoe-blacking.

SHOWY MADIA

Madia elegans

(Plate 26, fig. 3)

When blotched with crimson as they often are, the bright yellow heads of the showy madia look very like those of coreopsis, but the resemblance ends there, for the plants are stout and sticky instead of smooth and graceful. The characteristic tarweed odor is present, and although this is disagreeably suggestive of turpentine at close range, faint whiffs of it may be found spicily pleasant. The plants are common on hills, from southern California to Oregon and east to Nevada, but they make no great show of bloom owing to their habit of flowering in the evening and sleeping in the sunshine. If planted in the shade in the garden, the flowers will remain open all day.

The name madia is unusual in that it is of Chilian origin instead of classical, and this is due to the fact that the best known species (Madia sativa) is native to Chili. This furnishes an oil which is used abroad in cooking and is declared by many travelers to be superior in taste to olive oil.

ARNICA

Arnica cordifolia

(Plate 26, fig. 4)

The flowering heads of arnica are borne singly on hairy stems usually about a foot tall, and have bright yellow toothed rays and darker yellow centers. The involucres are rather deep and hairy, and the leaves in this species generally more or less conventionally heart-shaped. This is taken note of in the specific term cordifolia, which means heart-shaped, while the velvety texture of the leaves is referred to by the Greek for lamb's skin, which is the word for the genus.

The arnica illustrated grows in open woods in the mountains of California, north to British Columbia and east to Colorado, but it is the narrower leaved mountain arnica (Arnica montana) from which the soothing lotion is derived.

BUSH SENECIO

SENECIO DOUGLASI

(Plate 26, fig. 5)

The bush senecio is a shrubby perennial, usually three or four feet high, which occupies plains and hills in the West and climbs warm slopes in California to an altitude of 5000 feet. Since it blooms in such locations as late as December, it is frequently conspicuous when other flowers are scarce. The finely cut foliage is covered with a coating of white hairs. It is this gray and hoary appearance that has probably given the name for the genus, since senecio is fashioned from the Latin word for old man. There is some disagreement as to this, however, for one authority claims that it is the shining white hairs of the pappus that are hoary looking and another that when the flowers have fallen from their places of attachment to the disk, the latter resembles a bald head.

CALIFORNIA SENECIO

SENECIO CALIFORNICUS

(Plate 26, fig. 6)

The queer dwarf-like forms of the California senecio which grow on the strand look very different from the tall slender ones to be found in the shade of other herbage on the hilltop. The former are bunchy, an inch and a half tall, with but a few flower-heads that are absurdly large by contrast, while the latter are two feet or more in height, slender and unbranched, with but one head. These smooth little annuals with lance-shaped leaves are confined to southern California, but are quite able to adapt themselves to the sand-dunes along the shore as well as to dry places in the valleys and foothills, especially if the soil is somewhat sandy. The bright-yellow flowers appear in February and continue to bloom until May.

WOOLLY ERIOPHYLLUM

Eriophyllum lanatum

(Plate 27, fig. 1)

The woolly eriophyllum is an attractive plant with many golden flower-heads on slender stalks, dark-green leaves and a covering of white wool on the underside of leaves, buds and stems. This white down is so characteristic of all the different forms as to be noted in the names of both the genus and the species. The former is from Greek words meaning woolly-leaf and the latter from the Latin for woolly.

Hillsides, from coast to mountain and in the Yosemite, are the localities in which one may find this cheery little perennial.

GOLDEN ERIOPHYLLUM

Eriophyllum confertiflorum

(Plate 27, fig. 2)

The small yellow flower-heads of the golden eriophyllum are closely crowded into flat-topped clusters like those of some goldenrods. The stems are covered with the white down characteristic of the genus, and as they frequently occur in clumps, the masses of bloom are often strikingly beautiful. The plants are bushy perennials with woody bases and are found commonly in the hills and mountains of the lower part of the chaparral in central and southern California; occasionally also on warm, rocky slopes in the Yosemite below 6500 feet. They are sometimes called golden-yarrow, though the true yarrow (Achillea millefolium) belongs to a different tribe of the aster family.

Plate 27

ASTER FAMILY

1
2
3
4
5
6
7

PINCUSHIONS

Chænactis glabriuscula

(Plate 27, fig. 3)

The golden heads of pincushions have an outer row or two of scalloped flowers arranged like a double ruffle around a soft cushiony center. This is smooth before the disk-flowers open, but looks as though stuck full of golden pins as the narrow tubes elongate. The flower stalks are long and slender, arising from a basal tuft of prettily cut leaves. Although covered with white wool at first, they lose this as they grow older and then become smooth and green.

From April to June these charming plants may be found in the lower hills and along the coast of middle and southern California. They are partial to loose sandy soil or somewhat rocky ground, but when growing in the shade of taller herbs or grasses they may become tall and slender or show other variations, which are sometimes recognized as named forms. There are several white-flowered species of chænactis, so like this yellow one as to be easily known as near relatives.

The scientific name is formed from Greek words meaning gaping-ray and this refers to the appearance of the marginal flowers of some of the species.

BÆRIA

Bæria chrysostoma

(Plate 27, fig. 4)

Massed on cliffs near the shore, bæria forms a cloth-of-gold, varied here and there with the paler yellow of evening-primroses, the glowing orange of California poppies, yellow tidy-tips and senecios, and embroidered at the edges with lavender phacelias and white popcorn flowers. In the spring, foothill slopes and plains are often so thickly clothed with bæria blossoms that shoes become golden with the pollen.

Although thriving best in moist ground throughout the Golden State, nothing daunts this hardy little annual. Where there is plenty of water in the soil, the plants may grow a foot tall and bear large heads, but when pressed for moisture on hard rocky trails, they do well to become an inch and a half tall and are much bunched, with tiny leaves and heads less than one-fourth of an inch across. On the strand similar dwarfs will produce heads three times as large, while such plants as become stunted through competition with the grasses will remain unbranched and slender with thread-like leaves and stems and tiny heads.

VENEGASIA

VENEGASIA CARPESIOIDES

(Plate 27, fig. 5)

Like miniature suns with bright-yellow centers and many paler yellow rays, the heads of venegasia droop slightly at the ends of red-brown branches. The long-pointed light-green leaves, with toothed edges, cluster thickly about the scattered heads and along the woody stems. These shrubs are of unusual beauty, but are limited to shady canyons and stream-banks in southern California and are in consequence not as well known as they should be. The genus is named in honor of a Jesuit missionary, Venegas.

GAILLARDIA

GAILLARDIA ARISTATA

(Plate 27, fig. 6)

Gaillardias, with their wealth of bloom and gorgeous coloring, are familiar sights on western plains and in gardens everywhere. The centers are usually orange or orange-red, while the rays run the gamut of yellows from pure canary to deeper yellow blotched with crimson at the base. In the larger heads the ray-flowers may be an inch and a half long, making these splendid specimens into setting suns of glowing color.

Not only are gaillardias more than satisfactory in the garden, where they put forth a succession of flowers all summer long and late into the autumn, but they are well adapted to cutting if there are vases or bowls to be filled with bloom.

On southern plains, from Louisiana west to Arizona, the rose-ring gaillardia (Gaillardia pulchella) is startling in its vivid coloring. The tips of the rays are yellow, but for most of their length they are a rich reddish-purple, so that wherever the plants occur in any abundance they are visible from a long distance as great splotches of color. The plants grow especially well on the plains of Texas, where they furnish large quantities of yellow honey that is greatly esteemed.

LASTHENIA

Lasthenia glabrata

(Plate 27, fig. 7)

Resembling its close relative, bæria, but with larger heads, lasthenia spreads beautiful yellow sheets of bloom over ground that is low and wet. It is not at all averse to a moderate amount of alkali in its water supply and finding this quite to its taste in salt marshes along the coast, may frequently be found in such localities.

The pretty name Lasthenia is given in honor of a Greek maiden who attended the lectures of Plato attired like a man.

WESTERN THISTLE

Carduus occidentalis

(Plate 28, fig. 1)

The western thistle forms stately groups of tall branching plants with crimson flowers so long and slender that they seem to rise from their gray involucres like flames from a brazier. Guarded against spoliation by their armoring of sharp spines, protected against drouth by their cobwebby covering of white hairs, they march triumphantly from coast to desert and from Lower California to southern Oregon, taking possession of sandy soil and thriving with little encouragement. Some thistles are of limited use, but the two famous members of the family are the blessed thistle (Carduus benedictus), which furnishes a drug, and the artichoke (Cynara scolymus), the buds of which appear on the table as a mound of thick, olive-green leaves and are eaten as a salad.

Plate 28

ASTER FAMILY

1
3
5
7
6
2
4

The earliest mention of the thistle is in Genesis, where it is spoken of as the curse of Adam's land after his expulsion from the Garden of Eden. Many farmers of today, all over the world, also find the thistle a troublesome weed and one difficult to eradicate. On the other hand it is not without honors. It is said to be the oldest national flower on record, tradition ascribing its adoption as such by Scotland in the middle of the thirteenth century. The legend relates that in 1263 the Danish army landed unobserved on the coast of Scotland, and although accustomed to regarding a night attack as unwarrior-like, was so sorely tempted by the proximity of the Scottish troops encamped nearby, as to disregard this rule. They began creeping noiselessly and unobserved towards the sleeping enemy and success seemed within their grasp when one of the soldiers set his bare foot upon a thistle. His sharp cry of pain was the signal for an alarm which roused the camp and the Scots fell upon the Danes, defeating them with terrible slaughter. Since that day the thistle has been regarded as the national emblem of Scotland. It appears on the arms and banners of the country with the motto: "No one may attack me with impunity," and in the reign of James II it was officially recognized on the coinage of the realm. Visitors to Scotland today will find the emblem of the thistle appearing at every turn and in every guise, from embroidery to jewelry.

In northern Europe during the early days of legend and hero worship, the thistle was considered sacred to the great god Thor, since the bright color of the blossoms was derived from the lightning which formed his weapon. This idea led to its being credited with magical powers and able not only to protect from destruction by lightning, but to cure all imaginable ills. An ancient writer remarks of the blessed thistle: "It helpeth swimmings and giddiness of the head, or the disease called vertigo. It is an excellent remedy against the yellow jaundice and other infirmities of the gall. It strengthens the attractive faculties in man and clarifies the blood. The continual drinking of the decoction of it helps red faces, tetters and ringworm. It helps the plague, sores, boils and itch, the bitings of mad dogs and venomous beasts. It strengthens the memory and cures deafness." Today the bitter substance present in the blessed thistle is used only as a tonic, especially among Europeans.

The Latin name carduus has been derived from a Celtic word meaning point and refers to the spiny-pointed leaves of the different species. The word thistle is connected with the teasel (Dipsacus fullonum), which belongs to a related group. The recurved hard and elastic bracts of this plant were used by clothiers for teasing cloth so as to raise the nap on it. From this has come the meaning of teasing as worrying or annoying.

STAR-THISTLE

Centaurea melitensis

(Plate 28, fig. 2)

While a single plant of the star thistle may please with a resemblance to a branched candalabrum holding globes of yellow flame in vase-shaped involucres, too close a contact reveals the presence of vicious spines that pierce and stab. From July to November these weeds appropriate the fields and waysides of California and Arizona. They are considered only a little less obnoxious than a close relative (Centaurea solstitialis), which has longer spines and takes extensive areas in Northern and Central California. Both are natives of Europe that have emigrated to this country and become completely naturalized in the far West, where they are considered good honey-plants. The former yields a light amber honey of good flavor, in Sacramento county during May and June, while the latter produces a heavy white honey of cloying sweetness and a greenish-yellow tinge. The yield is from July first to frost and may average twenty or thirty tons a season.

Many species of Centaurea are favorites in the garden. The best known, perhaps, are dusty miller (Centaurea cineraria), with golden-yellow or purple heads and white-woolly foliage, sweet sultan (Centaurea moschata) and bachelor-buttons (Centaurea cyanus), which appears as a weed in European wheat-fields, but produces a number of beautiful varieties under cultivation. It is this species that was named Centaurea after the centaur, Chiron. The legend relates that when his foot was accidentally wounded by an arrow of Hercules, a plant with blue blossoms immediately sprang up and its root was successfully used to heal the wound. The star thistle causes wounds with its sharp spines rather than heals them, as is indicated by this common name, which harks back to a weapon of war used in mediæval times and called "morning-star." This consisted of a metal ball set with murderous spikes and mounted on a long handle. Its resemblance to the round involucres of the star thistle, set with projecting spines, explains the origin of the name.

HYPOCHŒRIS

Hypochœris radicata

(Plate 28, fig. 3)

Many of our commonest and hardiest weeds are gay adventurers, ready to leave ancestral homes and travel abroad. So it is that the plumy bristles attached to the seeds of Hypochœris have carried them far and wide, and some of those that found a lodging place in cargoes being put aboard the freighters of European ports, eventually became established in the ballast of New York and Philadelphia. From there they have journeyed by whatever means offered, until reaching the Pacific Coast, they have made themselves very much at home in field and wayside.

The resemblance of the flowering heads of hypochœris to those of its near relative the dandelion, is apparent, but the strange name that is formed from words meaning "for a pig" becomes clear only when it is known that the plants are considered edible by this omnivorous animal.

MALACOTHRIX

Malacothrix californica

(Plate 28, fig. 4)

The lovely flowers of malacothrix, borne on tall leafless stalks, look like copies of the common dandelion, but they are far more stately and aristocratic than their lowly cousin. The heads are considerably larger—two inches in diameter as a rule—and composed of several hundred ribbon-like flowers crowded together into a fluffy rosette. The buds hang like lemon-colored balls on curved stems. The finely cut leaves are gathered together at the base of the stalk into a pretty tuft which wears when young a covering of soft white hairs. These are referred to in the Greek malacothrix, which means soft hair.

This species of Malacothrix is found blooming from March to May in open ground and sandy soil, from the Sacramento Valley to San Diego, and is especially common along the coast and in the interior valleys. The hairs disappear as the plants grow older and then the latter are scarcely to be distinguished from the form (Malacothrix glabrata) that is at home on the dry eastern portion of the Sierra Nevada in California and Nevada, and as far east and south as Utah and Arizona.

WILD LETTUCE

LACTUCA PULCHELLA

(Plate 28, fig. 5)

This wild-flower sister of the cultivated lettuce, with its lance-shaped leaves and many flower-heads—yellow-centered and with blue-lavender rays—is always charming, while the garden variety loses its attraction as soon as the succulent leaves give way to the clumsy stalk of inconspicuous yellow flowers. The wild lettuce is not confined to the garden for the sake of edible leaves or stem, but seeks open pine forests in the California and Nevada mountains or open valleys in the northern part of the country. A few other wild species of lettuce are as pretty as this one, but the majority have inconspicuous flowers and are common weeds. The prickly lettuce (Lactuca scariola) attracts notice by the peculiar position of its leaves. Instead of standing out from the stem horizontally in order to make the most of the sunlight, they turn their edges upward and the surfaces vertical, in the manner of other so-called "compass-plants."

All species of lettuce have a bitter and acrid juice with a milky appearance as it exudes from broken parts of the plants. The name lactuca is formed from the Latin word for milk. This juice is extracted from certain species and used as a narcotic and sedative. It is said to have an effect similar to that of opium but less likely to produce untoward results.

AGOSERIS

AGOSERIS RETRORSA

(Plate 28, fig. 6)

Agoseris plainly shows its relationship to the dandelion in its yellow head of strap-shaped flowers and the similar appearance of the rosette of leaves at the base of the flower stalk. The lobes of the leaves are usually turned downward, and when the plants are young, both stem and leaf are covered with a light wool. This disappears with age so that it cannot be depended upon as a distinguishing characteristic at all times. The agoseris of our western plains (Agoseris glauca) has smooth green leaves, although the involucre beneath the large bright-yellow head is often covered with white wool. The common species of the prairies (Agoseris cuspidata) is a harbinger of spring, and is often called false-dandelion.

CHICORY

CICHORIUM INTYBUS

(Plate 28, fig. 7)

Many-pointed like radiant stars, ethereal blue like the sky, a galaxy of chicory blossoms will transform many a lush green brook-bank or grassy roadside into a strange new firmament. Instead of crowding scores or hundreds of flowers into a solid mass like the dandelion and other near relatives, there are scarcely more than a score in a chicory-head, each with a broad fringed ray. The center of the group is creamy white and the stamen column dark-blue, in attractive contrast to the paler lavender-blue of the encircling rays. If the stems are cut and placed in water, one or two new heads will spread its delicate rays each day for ten days or two weeks and supply an artistic bouquet in the Japanese style.

Probably the jaunty air of the blossoms and their color have combined to suggest the name of blue sailors, but the usual term has a longer history and a polyglot origin. "Chicory" is the English form of cichorium, which in turn is said to be an Arabic name latinized, as well as the Egyptian term adopted by the Greeks.

Like most of our common weeds, chicory has come over from Europe, and after gaining a foothold in Massachusetts, where it was brought from Holland in 1785, it has spread far and wide. It has even become such a troublesome weed in some localities as to have called forth a bulletin by the Department of Agriculture which deals with methods of control and eradication. On the other hand, it is grown in certain parts of this country for commercial purposes and abroad it is an important article of trade. Not only are the leaves edible when blanched or young and tender, but they afford excellent fodder for sheep. It is to the long perennial tap-root, however, that chicory owes its greatest value. This is roasted, powdered and mixed with coffee or used entirely in place of the latter, especially abroad. England imports as much as five thousand tons a year, while as long ago as 1860 France was using sixteen million pounds annually. During and since the World War its consumption has increased enormously even in this country. As a honey-plant chicory has received some attention since it yields both pollen and honey over a long period of summer blooming.

The garden endive (Chicorium endiva), with curly peppery leaves which are used in salads, is also a chicory, while a somewhat more distant relative (Tragopogon porrifolius), furnishes a root with a flavor like that of oysters instead of the fragrant coffee-berry.

LILY FAMILY

Liliaceæ

The lilies are spread all over the world except in the Arctic Zone. They are especially rich in choice ornamentals of which the chief perhaps is the tulip in an immense number of varieties, colors and double forms. Tulip culture is a passion with some amateurs, as well as a profitable business. The true lilies also exhibit a wide range of form and color, but they are not as extensively grown in gardens as their beauty and ease of cultivation warrant. Hyacinths combine a sweet fragrance with flowers of many colors, and the lily-of-the-valley is famed for its delicate odor and dainty bell-flowers. Squills, day-lilies, asphodels, dracænas, and ornithogalums all have their admirers and are extensively cultivated, while the mariposas, erythroniums, trilliums, native lilies and brodiæas are among the most eagerly sought and loved of wild-flowers.

A number of the lily family are medicinal, while asparagus and the many species and varieties of onion are important as food or relishes. Of these the garlic has been known and cultivated since earliest times, and grows wild in Sicily, Italy and the South of France. It has such a strong flavor that merely rubbing the salad bowl with a tiny piece of the bulb is sufficient to flavor the entire salad. The extracted oil has been found useful both internally and externally as a mild stimulant, and when it is combined with camphor it becomes the prophylactic known as Thieves' Vinegar. The dried outer skin of the common onion yields an excellent yellow dye, and the bulbs of this genus appear in the market under the names of shallot, leek, false-leek, rocambole and chives.

FIRECRACKER FLOWER

Brodiæa coccinea

(Plate 29, fig. 1)

As far as color and shape are concerned, a cluster of firecracker flowers attached to the main stem by slender pedicels look so much like a bunch of small firecrackers fastened by their fuses that they might well furnish a perfectly safe and sane Fourth of July celebration. It would be a pity, however, to bring these charming little wildings in from their haunts on grassy hillsides or in open forests where their crimson blossoms serve a better purpose. An unusual color combination is afforded by the green of the corolla-lobes encircling the creamy white, petal-like stamens in the throat of the bright-crimson tube.

It is only in southern Oregon and northern California that the firecracker flower finds itself at home although, when transplanted

Plate 29

LILY FAMILY

1
2
3
4
5
6
7

to suitable spots in the garden, it will grow remarkably tall and produce an abundance of bloom that keeps its beauty indefinitely when transferred to a vase.

ITHURIEL'S SPEAR

Brodiæa laxa

(Plate 29, fig. 2)

Fancifully likened to the spear borne by the Angel Ithuriel, because of its straight slimness of stem, this brodiæa joins its twin-sister, the harvest brodiæa (Brodiæa grandiflora) in beautifying grasslands from early summer until the hay is ready for cutting. The differences between the two are so slight as to be of little general interest since these concern mainly the number of stamens: the latter having but three and the former the usual six. Both have beautiful, large purple blossoms in loose clusters that are very showy and among the best for home culture. They are found commonly in fields and open woodlands and on grassy hillsides, from central California northward through Oregon and Washington, where the bulbs are roasted and eaten by the Indians.

BLUE BRODIÆA

Brodiæa capitata

(Plate 29, fig. 3)

The blue brodiæa is one of the best-known and most widely distributed of the many beautiful California flowers that bloom in the spring. It may be found abundantly everywhere on clay slopes and hills of the coast districts and even climbing up into the pine-belt of the Sierra Nevada and Yosemite. Owing to the frequence and wide distribution of the plants, they vary greatly in size. Some are but a few inches tall with tiny flowers, where the soil is dry and hard, while those in the shelter of the shrubs of the chaparral may stretch up to a height of several feet. The lovely blossoms vary, even in the same cluster, from rose-lavender to blue-lavender and resemble hyacinths in form. They may be cut and kept fresh indefinitely, forming especially attractive bouquets when combined with feathery grasses. When gathering them care should be taken not to damage the underground parts or destroy the foliage. The fibrous-coated corms from which the flowering stalks spring, are dug with difficulty from the hard, clay soil but are relished by Indians and children for their nutty flavor.

GOLDEN-STARS

BLOOMERIA AUREA

(Plate 29, fig. 4)

The large, loose clusters of these narrow-petaled blossoms are placed so airily on slender, leafless stems as to look like showers of golden stars. The individual flower is very like that of the golden brodiæa (Brodiæa ixioides, fig. 5) but is more star-like, since the segments of the perianth are separate and wide-spreading instead of united into a tube at the base. Golden-stars is not the mountain climber that the golden brodiæa is, but sprinkles the mesas and foothills of southern California with bright blossoms from April to June. They should be planted in the home garden in the sunshine, in warm, sandy, well-drained soil.

GOLDEN BRODIÆA

BRODIÆA IXIOIDES

(Plate 29, fig. 5)

The six-pointed, star-shaped blossoms of the golden brodiæa form loose, open clusters on slender stems which may be but a few inches tall or shoot up to more than a foot in height. The flowers are bright-yellow, veined with brown and differ from golden-stars (Bloomeria aurea, fig. 4), which they very closely resemble, in the united corolla and stamens attached to broad filaments, instead of slender, thread-like ones, that rise from a tiny cup. They may be looked for during the summer in the mountains from southern California to Oregon where they often reach an altitude of 8500 feet. At still higher levels a very similar plant (Brodiæa gracilis) may be distinguished by its smaller size and thread-like filaments to the stamens. The white brodiæa (Brodiæa hyacinthina), although also common in the mountains, confines itself to low moist soil and may be found in the Yosemite.

NODDING ONION

Allium cernuum

(Plate 29, fig. 6)

The pretty cluster of rose-lavender blossoms of the nodding onion closely resembles that of the familiar onion of the garden, and the odor from crushed leaves and bulbs is also similar. The individual flowers rise and bend on slender pedicels as they perform the work of the day. They are concerned solely with having available a fresh supply of pollen and nectar to satisfy their insect friends—butterflies, honey-bees and especially bumble-bees. These must come again and again, for, although the nectar is always flowing, the stamens push forth one by one from the enfolding petals and sepals; each in turn sheds its pollen and then shrivels. The young buds hang downward, but rise slowly as the flower unfolds until the ripening capsule, surrounded by the remains of the shriveled perianth, stands stiffly upright.

This wild onion thrives best in the cool air of the mountains of Oregon, northwards and in the Rockies. In the Middle West, the flowers of the common wild onion (Allium mutabile) were abundant enough in the early days, before the prairie flora disappeared in front of advancing civilization, to furnish an important source of honey. They were reported to be so abundant in 1878 on the prairies around Chicago as to form an unbroken carpet of delicate pink bloom. This was a busy time for the bees, whose myriad wings ventilated the hives so well that, by the time the honey had ripened, the original onion-flavor had entirely disappeared. The honey was then considered equal in taste and appearance to that gleaned from the white clover.

The Latin name allium is derived from a Celtic word meaning hot or burning and refers to the acrid taste and pungent odor, so characteristic of the onion and its near relatives.

PURPLE ONION

ALLIUM FIMBRIATUM

(Plate 29, fig. 7)

Of the thirty species of onion on the Pacific Coast, this purple-flowered one stands out as one of the most decorative in appearance, since the clusters of blossoms are unusually large and vividly colored. The perianth segments are more pointed than are those of the nodding onion, but the flower structure is similar and the characteristic odor present in leaves and bulbs. The plants occupy stony slopes in the chaparral belt of southern California, toward the desert and away from the coast.

The swamp onion (Allium validum) of wet places above the middle altitudes in the mountains is a satisfactory substitute for the cultivated onion. Another species (Allium campanulatum), frequent on dry slopes in the mountains, is small and bears flowers of a pale rose-color. A pink or red species (Allium serratum) and a white one (Allium hæmatochiton), with large, showy clusters of flowers, are attractive scattered throughout the chaparral and grassland of southern California.

SHOWY MARIPOSA

CALOCHORTUS VENUSTUS

(Plate 30, fig. 1)

Like a swarm of bright butterflies are these mariposas as they flutter under the caress of the breeze. The petals bear many colors—from white to lilac and deep wine-red—with spots and blotches of contrasting tints. White-petaled forms with dark-brown spots rimmed in pale-yellow stand side by side with those that are a pure lavender blotched with maroon, while close at hand are dark purplish-red flowers marked with still deeper shades and banded with yellow.

The pretty name mariposa is Spanish for butterfly, which so aptly describes these charming blossoms. The name calochortus is formed from Greek words meaning handsome-grass and refers to the narrow, grass-like leaves. Nearly every species of the genus is under cultivation to some extent and no garden is complete without some of the varieties.

LILAC MARIPOSA

Calochortus splendens

(Plate 30, fig. 2)

Surrounded by waving grasses, the lilac mariposa bears aloft its rose-lavender chalice on slender stem, or folds delicate petals in the coolness of late afternoon or on a cloudy day. Within the lovely cup, the purplish-blue of six large stamens adds a final touch of distinction to its fragile beauty.

Grassy or bushy hills of central and southern California offer this species a home in the open places, while another lilac-flowered mariposa (Calochortus nuttalli) is distributed more widely. This climbs the mountains into the Yosemite and higher, or travels eastward through Arizona and Utah, and is the official flower of the latter state, where its corms furnished food to the early Mormons as they crossed the desert.

YELLOW MARIPOSA

Calochortus luteus

(Plate 30, fig. 3)

The yellow mariposa varies in tint from a clear yellow to the deeper orange shades, or even becomes cream-white or pale-violet. It is capricious also in ornamenting the petals with spots or blotches, for these may be brown in the yellow forms, maroon or crimson in the lilac ones, or variously colored in still others.

When in flower, these golden lily-cups appear abundantly in dry or gravelly ground of the Coast Ranges and Sierra foothills of central California, although in the latter situations the vari-colored blossoms are more frequent than the pure-yellow ones. The corms are often dug and eaten either raw or cooked and are said to have a sweet, nutty flavor and to be very nutritious.

In the deserts of California and Arizona, there is an orange-colored mariposa (Calochortus kennedyi) that is incredibly bril-

Plate 30

LILY FAMILY

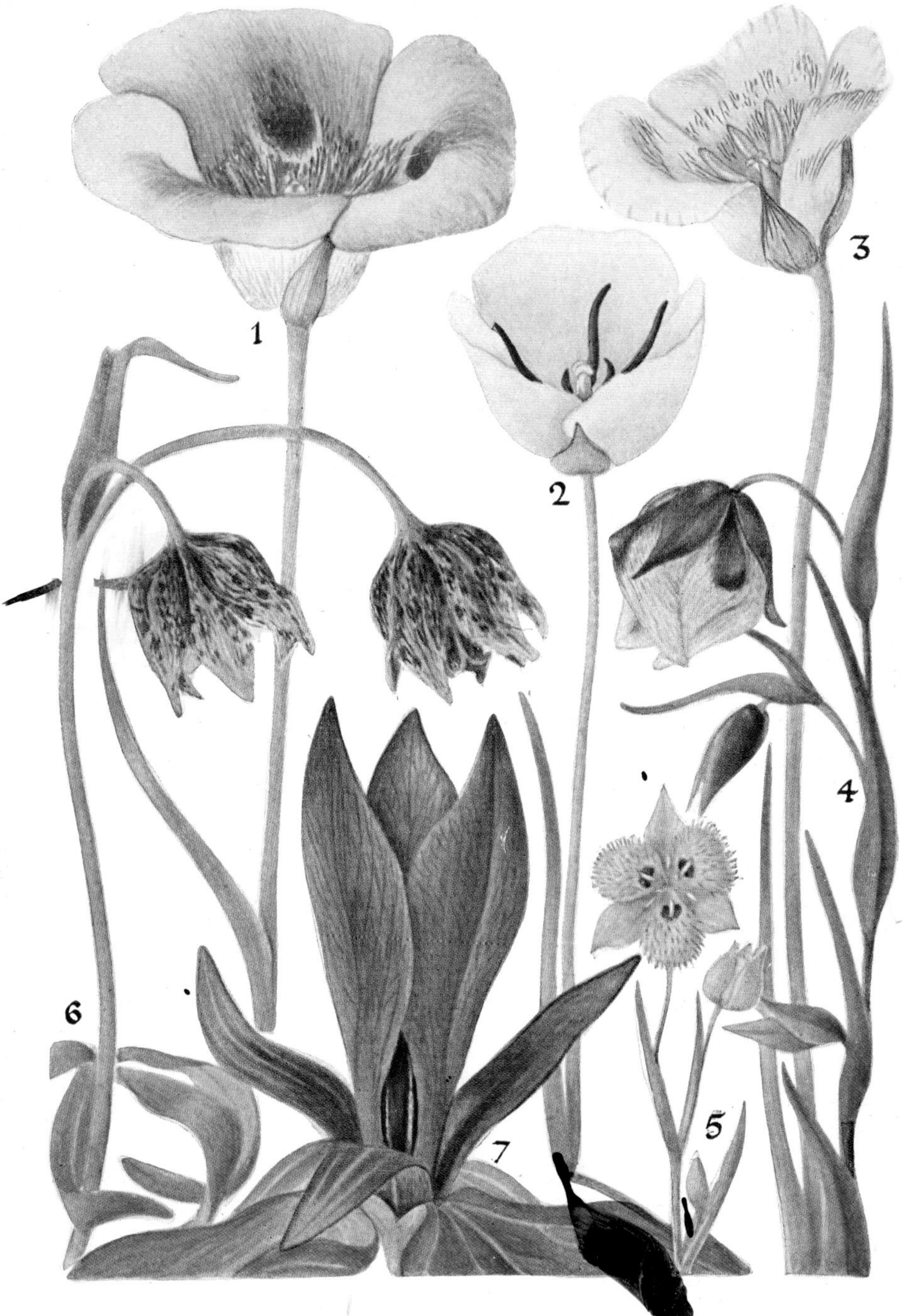
1
2
3
4
5
6
7

liant in hue and especially gorgeous in its barren setting. Each blossom wears a coat of many colors: the sepals are pale-green, pink and orange, the petals peach-tinted without, orange-vermilion within where they are ornamented with purplish honey-glands covered with vermilion hairs. In a favorable season, these flaming flowers may cover foothills and desert floor by the thousand.

FAIRY-LANTERN

Calochortus albus rubellus

(Plate 30, fig. 4)

Exquisitely dainty, the shining globes of the fairy-lantern seem to float like irridescent soap-bubbles. The satiny-white petals, flushed with old-rose, curve to form globular blossoms that are airily pendant on slender stems. The pure-white flowers of the species itself (Calochortus albus), which are much commoner than this variety, are set off by pale-greenish sepals and a light-green swollen gland at the base of each petal. The variety is purple-tinged throughout with veinings in deeper shades of the same lovely color. The golden fairy-lantern (Calochortus pulchellus) with pendant yellow globes, completes the charming trio. All three make their homes in central California, preferably in open woods and shady slopes in the mountains.

YELLOW PUSSY-EARS

Calochortus monophyllus

(Plate 30, fig. 5)

The fuzzy pointed petals of this mariposa, with their alert erectness, are individually very suggestive of the sensitive upstanding ears of a yellow kitten, and, when they are combined in threes with pale-yellow sepals between, a most quaint and dainty blossom is the result. They are not at all common, but may be found here and there in the pine-belt of the Sierra Nevada, where they bloom in the spring.

There is also a white pussy-ears (Calochortus maweanus) which may be varied by a pale-lilac tint to the petals themselves or to the hairs that cover them. The warmth of early spring brings forth these furry, little blossoms quite abundantly in moist places of the Coast Ranges and foothills of the Sierra Nevada, from central California northward to Oregon.

MISSION-BELLS

Fritillaria lanceolata

(Plate 30, fig. 6)

These bronze bells, mottled with purple and dull yellowish-green, hang downward from bending stalks, and what looks like a clapper, fashioned to bring forth musical resonance, is but the pendant style, cleft into three spreading lobes. The odd checquerings of green and yellow against the bronze of this unusual blossom have been noted in the Latin name fritillaria, which means chess-board or dice-box, and the species often goes by the name of brown fritillary.

These unique flowers are to be found quite abundantly on coastal hillsides and in woodlands, from central California to British Columbia and eastward to western Idaho. The most popular of the frittilaries under cultivation are the checquered-lily (Fritillaria meleagris) and the crown-imperial (Fritillaria imperialis). The former has short, open bell-flowers checquered and veined with purple or maroon on a paler ground, and the latter purple, brick-red or yellow-red blossoms.

PURPLE TRILLIUM

Trillium sessile

(Plate 30, fig. 7)

Wherever found—east, west, north or south—in woodland or on hillside, the trilliums are among the earliest messengers of spring. They are sometimes so early, indeed, as to precede that early bird of spring, the robin, and to be called wake-robin in consequence. As purely white as the snow-bank which it succeeds, is the wake-robin of the Middle West (Trillium nivale); white, changing to pink are the flowers of the fragrant wake-robin (Trillium ovatum) that gleam in the cool shade of mountain brook-banks of the Northwest; and reddish-purple those of the purple trilliums (Trillium erectum and T. sessile) of the East and West.

The purple trillium illustrated, which grows in California woodlands, appears as a greenish-yellow or white form north of San Francisco, but southward, the three long narrow petals are richly rose-purple in coloring, with darker veinings. The purple trillium (Trillium erectum) of the East and Northeast, bears flowers of a similar color on a slender stalk above the three leaves, the petals curving back with age. This is known as a carrion-flower, a name that seems to be justified by the number of flies attracted as pollen carriers. The reddish berries are nauseous and the roots, which have been used by the Indians and early settlers as an astringent and local irritant in skin diseases, are violently emetic.

The name trillium means triple and this number refers, not only to sepals, petals and pistil, but to the stem-leaves also. The plants are among the choicest of spring bloomers and when transferred to the garden should be planted in rich, moist soil. They may be propagated from seed, but, since it takes two or three years for them to come into flower, it is better to transplant them, and, once established, a colony will last for years.

WILD TIGER LILY

Lilium humboldti

(Plate 31, fig. 1)

A straight stem, eight feet tall, hung with a score or more of large brilliant blossoms and whorls of lance-shaped leaves, combine to make the wild tiger lily a stately and handsome plant. The many bright reddish-orange flowers, gaily ornamented with dark-purple spots, are unusually beautiful, not only in coloring but in form, as the six ribbon-like parts of the blossom recurve gracefully and reveal pendant red anthers and a yellow-green style.

This lily grows wild in canyons of the southern California mountains and in dry open places in the northern portion of the Sierra Nevada, but it will respond to cultivation and furnish strik-

Plate 31

LILY FAMILY

1
2
3
4
5
6
7

ing effects. There are many superb lilies suitable for garden culture, but comparatively few are grown and of these the tiger lily (Lilium tigrinum) and the madonna lily (Lilium candidum) are the best-known.

The name lilium is formed from a Celtic word signifying whiteness and nearly all the legends and historical references concern the white lily, although the distinction of being considered more gorgeously arrayed than "Solomon in all his glory" belongs to the bright orange-red lily of the fields of Galilee. The madonna lily (Lilium candidum) has such waxy-white petals as to have become the emblem of purity and beauty. It was consequently dedicated to the Virgin Mary by the Christians and to the goddess Hera by the Greeks. The ancient Jews believed that the madonna lily possessed the power of warding off witchcraft and enchantments and so Judith crowned herself with a wreath of these flowers when she undertook her dangerous errand to the tent of Holofernes.

It is this same lily that furnished the early motifs in architecture and design as illustrated by the "lily-work" on the tops of the pillars in Solomon's temple and in the design for the royal crown. Centuries later, each of the thirty-eight knights of the Order of the Lily wore a silver lily attached to a chain of gold interlaced with the letter M. The initial stood for Mary and the order was devoted to the service of the Virgin, in deeds of charity and in purity of living. It was originally instituted in 1048 by Garcia, King of Navarre, in recognition of a miraculous recovery from sickness, after he had dreamed of the Madonna emerging from one of the white lilies in the garden of the palace. Four centuries later, Ferdinand of Aragon established a similar order, the members of which were likewise sworn to the service of the Virgin.

In the days of heraldry and warring factions, the lily was emblazoned on the shield of Normandy and the rose on that of England. It was customary to call the Prince of Wales, the "rose of expectancy" and the Dauphin the "lily of France." In the strife between the Guelphs and the Ghibellines, from the 11th to the 14th centuries, the former adopted the red lily as their badge and the latter the white one, just as the English Houses of York and Lancaster were known by the white and red roses.

LEOPARD LILY

Lilium pardalinum

(Plate 31, fig. 2)

The bright, orange-red blossoms of the leopard lily nod on slender pedicels above the level of the surrounding vegetation, their exotic beauty seeming all the more striking in contrast with the dark-green of the background. There may be as many as twenty-five flowers on a single plant although the usual number is fewer than this. The sepals and petals, conspicuously marked with large purplish-brown spots, curve gracefully backwards and reveal the protruding style and six stamens with large, reddish-brown anthers.

These beautiful plants prefer damp places in the mountains, such as shady stream-banks and half-boggy meadows, from central California north to British Columbia; and they are an especially familiar sight along the Redwood Highway, in northern California and Oregon.

The Oregon lily (Lilium columbianum) resembles the leopard lily, but the flowers are smaller and the color more variable. This is common in the valley of the Hood River but somewhat less frequent from northern California to British Columbia.

CHAPARRAL LILY

Lilium rubescens

(Plate 31, fig. 3)

Not only do the lovely clusters of the chaparral lily exhibit a charming range of color from the white of unopened buds, through the coral-pink of full-blown flowers to the reddish-purple of fading blossoms, but they also exhale a fragrance that is not the least of their attractions. The Washington lily (Lilium washingtonianum) is similar. Though the flowers are somewhat larger, they too are pure white, turning purple with age, and very fragrant. They prefer the middle altitudes of the Sierra Nevada, in the forests and thickets, while the chaparral lily seeks the chaparral slopes of the Coast Ranges.

THIMBLE LILY

LILIUM BOLANDERI

(Plate 31, fig. 4)

This unobtrusive little plant hides itself in the mountains, and, far from emulating its more gorgeous and arrogant sisters, dresses demurely in sober colors and modestly hangs its head. The flowers of any one stalk may be few or many, horizontal or somewhat nodding, but they are all waxy-petaled and reddish-purple with dark-purple spots.

The plants are partial to plenty of moisture in the soil and inclined to take advantage of this in wet places about springs and in meadows, particularly in the Siskiyou Mountains of southern Oregon and northern California.

YELLOW LILY

LILIUM PARRYI

(Plate 31, fig. 5)

The stately plants of the yellow lily, hung with large, pale-yellow blossoms are among the finest specimens of the group and are quite easy to grow under cultivation. The traveler may see them frequently in moist places in the mountains of southern California, at the middle and upper altitudes. They are also especially abundant in some parts of the San Bernardino and San Jacinto Mountains.

The meadow lily (Lilium canadense) is a yellow lily of low meadows in the eastern half of the country, but is much deeper in color, ranging from dark-yellow to orange-yellow or red, and is spotted within with brownish dots. The segments spread more widely than do those of the yellow lily, or recurve, so that from tip to tip there may be a distance of two or three inches.

FAIRY LILY

LILIUM PARVUM

(Plate 31, fig. 6)

Although the fairy lily frequently grows but a foot or so tall and bears but two or three blossoms, it may shoot up to a height of six feet and produce thirty or more flowers at one time. They don a soberer tint of yellow than do many of its near relatives—a dull orange which merges into vermilion and is dotted with crimson or purple. Boggy places and moist stream-banks in the Sierra Nevada, up to 7000 feet, furnish favorable situations for this small-flowered lily.

GLACIER-LILY

ERYTHRONIUM PARVIFLORUM

(Plate 31, fig. 7)

Given early spring sunshine on mountain slopes and an abundance of clear cold water, seeping from surrounding snow-banks through porous soil, and the glacier-lily will spring up by the thousand and carpet the earth with smooth green leaves which can scarcely be seen for the myriad bright-yellow blossoms nodding above. On the slopes of Mount Rainier, they unite with the white avalanche-lily (Erythronium montanum) in turning the scene into fairyland. Although the glory of the mass soon passes, individuals may be found throughout the summer at higher and higher elevations where the late snows still linger.

About 5000 feet in the mountains of the coast and east to Utah, where open woods and grassy slopes are wet with melting snows or the seepage from brooks, the yellow fawn-lily (Erythronium grandiflorum) may be found. This has flowers very like those of the white fawn-lily (Erythronium californicum) of open hillsides, but the two pointed leaves are without the brown mottlings which suggest the markings of a fawn. The leaves of the pink fawn-lily (Erythronium revolutum) are also lightly mottled and its flowers unusually beautiful. This grows in woods somewhat inland from the coast, at fiom 500 to 2500 feet altitude and north to British Columbia. There are no red species of Erythronium on the Pacific Coast although this name is derived from the Greek word meaning red.

IRIS FAMILY

Iridaceæ

The irises should be classed with their close relatives the lilies on the one hand and the orchids on the other, as furnishing many of the most strikingly beautiful plants in existence. Besides the irises proper, which are being developed constantly by fanciers into more varied forms and unusual colors, the family comprises many lovely varieties of gladioli, freezias, crocuses and watsonias. These are to be distinguished from the closely related amaryllis family by the presence of three stamens instead of six, and the amaryllises are to be told from the lilies by the elevated corolla. Besides the amaryllis itself, this family numbers in its ranks many beautiful and fragrant blossoms such as the tuberose, narcissus, alstrœmeria, snowflake and snowdrop.

There are comparatively few of the iris family growing wild in America, but a great many in South Africa and Mexico. Among those of economic importance, the common blue flag furnishes an infusion that is used as a test for acids and alkalis, while those of the German blue iris are crushed, mixed with lime and used by painters under the name "iris-green." The seeds of the bog-iris serve as a substitute for coffee and the tubers of several South African species are eaten by the Hottentots. The familiar and fragrant orris-root powder is derived from an iris and has various uses, from that of a purgative when fresh, to that of entering into the composition of tooth-powders or perfume when dry.

RAINBOW IRIS

Iris hartwegi

(Plate 32, fig. 1)

Platoons of the rainbow iris unfurl lilac and yellow banners in the spring and cast them aside, one by one, in the march toward

Plate 32

IRIS FAMILY

ORCHID FAMILY

4
3
1
5
2

summer and maturity. These decorative plants of an erect and soldierly mien occupy open spaces in the evergreen forests of the middle altitudes, from the Siskiyous south through the Sierra Nevada to southern California. The flowers offer charming variety in coloring by combining yellow with lilac veining, or a pale lilac background with purple veins and a yellow spot placed for the guidance of bumble-bees.

Iris was the goddess of the storm and hence was represented by the rainbow. Since some of the early Greek species were celebrated for their rainbow brilliance of coloring, they were named in honor of the goddess. Irises are also frequently called flags, because of the banner-like nature of their floral parts. These stately blossoms were introduced centuries ago into Egyptian architecture, recognized by ancient Babylonia and Assyria as symbols of royalty and honored by the beauty-loving Japanese on every occasion.

The lily was early adopted as the badge of Normandy, but Louis VII chose the iris as his heraldic emblem when setting forth on a crusade. This has led to considerable confusion and discussion as to the original of the fleur-de-lys of present-day France. The French word for lily is "lis" and the iris was called the flower of Louis or the "fleur-de-Louis." This gradually became "fleur-de-luce" and finally "fleur-de-lys." So that it seems the "lilies of France" are actually irises, and it is the iris that appears on French emblems and coats-of-arms.

GRASS-IRIS

Sisyrinchium bellum

(Plate 32, fig. 2)

The purple six-pointed blossoms of the grass-iris transform hillsides as they open in the mornings and close in the afternoon. Each lives but one short day but is followed in such quick succession by others that the profusion each day is entirely new. The narrow grass-like leaves grow in bunches of varying size and height, from a few inches in dry situations to two feet where conditions are favorable. The flowers exhibit a wide range of coloring from pale-blue, through all the tints of lavender and lilac to dusky-purple with an occasional pure-white form. The slender point at the tip of each sepal and petal accentuates the starry effect and the yellow spot at the base guides visitors to the nectar glands.

Since this plant belongs to the iris family and not to the grasses, the name grass-iris is preferable to that of blue-eyed-grass commonly used. The long name of the genus Sisyrinchium is derived from words meaning pig and snout, since swine are said to grub the roots.

This grass-iris is common on moist grassy slopes near the coast, throughout California and resembles closely the smaller flowered species (Sisyrinchium angustifolium) of the Middle West and eastward. There is also a yellow grass-iris (Sisyrinchium californicum) to be found occasionally in wet places in the mountains of California and north to Oregon.

ORCHID FAMILY

ORCHIDACEÆ

Orchids are among the most irregular of flowers, often taking on such fantastic forms as to seem the product of the imagination instead of reality. Some resemble helmets or slippers, while others look curiously like beetles, bees or butterflies, and there is said to be one that resembles a little monkey. Not only are the shapes endlessly varied and unusual, but the differences in size, colors or combinations of colors are so great as to enable one authority to recognize over twelve thousand kinds, all different and yet each built on the same essential plan of flower structure. Tiny white orchids, less than an eighth of an inch long and looking like pearls strung along the green stem, bear the same family ear-marks as the strangely shaped and gorgeous specimens, six or eight inches long and of the most vivid hues.

This varied and complex group has developed a highly specialized mechanism for cross-pollination. Having made sure that the advertisement of color, size and form is sufficient to attract the attention of desirable insects, there remains the problem of loading the pollen for transfer to the stigma of another flower. Methods of accomplishing this are so certain among the orchids that most of them are able to reduce their supply of pollen to a minimum and usually possess but a single anther. The grooves, curves, spots and openings of the flower take part in guiding the visitor to his share in the process of fertilization. Some orchids have a lip so sensitive as to shut up suddenly when the insect alights, and hold it a prisoner until pollination is brought about. Sometimes it is the pollen masses that move when touched. These become fastened to the head of a bee by means of sticky disks, and then droop forward in such a way as to be deposited exactly on the stigma of the next flower visited.

The greater number of orchids that grow wild are inhabitants of tropical forests where they attach themselves to trees by means of long adventitious roots. In the temperate regions of the northern hemisphere, they take root in the earth. Although the culture of orchids is an extremely difficult occupation, it has become a passion in Europe during the last half-century. Rare specimens have sold for ten thousand dollars and more, while others have cost the lives of collectors who seek them among savage tribes or in forests that abound in wild beasts and poisonous snakes. Only a few are of any economic value but of these, several species of Vanilla, which supply a flavoring matter of the same name, are the most important.

YELLOW LADY-SLIPPER

Cypripedium parviflorum

(Plate 32, fig. 3)

Gleaming like golden balls in the dimness of northern forests or reflecting the dappled sunshine of aspen woodlands in the Rockies, the yellow lady-slipper is as beautiful as it is rare. The graceful stem and pretty leaves serve to set off effectively this quaint flower with inflated yellow pouch and twisted, streaming sepals of yellowish-green and crimson.

The name, cypripedium, means the sock or buskin of Venus and has reference to the oddly enlarged pouch-shaped petal, which the common name has modernized into lady-slipper.

This species of lady-slipper is found on the western coast only near Spokane, but occurs also here and there in moist woods from British Columbia to Nova Scotia, south to Nebraska and Georgia and in the Rockies. The mountain lady-slipper (Cypripedium montanum) is also quite rare but may be found in moist woods of the Sierra Nevada, from central California northwards and in the Coast Ranges. It has a white lip veined with purple. The California lady-slipper (Cypripedium californicum) is limited to swamps and moist ground in northern California. It has a somewhat pinker lip than the preceding species and shorter sepals that are greenish-yellow instead of purplish-brown.

STREAM-ORCHIS

Epipactis gigantea

(Plate 32, fig. 4)

The tall leafy stems of the stream-orchis stand gracefully outlined against dark banks of earth and bear towards their tips a row of small bronze and green blossoms, flushed with pink. This orchid has none of the arrogant beauty of exotic relatives, but seems unusually self-effacing by contrast. Like most of its kind it is not abundant, but blooms in spring and early summer on the banks of streams or around springs along the coast and east to Montana and Texas.

The name epipactis is from Greek words meaning to curdle milk, for which purpose the plant was probably early used. The helleborine (Epipactis latifolia), another species of the same genus as the stream-orchis, has a medicinal root formerly employed for the treatment of arthritic pains.

CALYPSO

Calypso borealis

(Plate 32, Fig. 5)

Exquisitely dainty, calypso hangs at the end of a rosy stem a lovely rose-purple slipper of about the size to fit a fairy's foot. The sepals and two of the petals form narrow twisted ribbons which flare upwards at the back, while the "toe" of the slipper is coquettishly ornamented with a yellow fuzz.

This fragrant little charmer hides in inaccessible bogs or blooms early in moist mountain woods. It prefers coolness to warmth and is found only in northern latitudes or at high altitudes. In the bogs of Maine to Minnesota and northward to 68 degrees; in the mountains of Oregon, Washington and Colorado, as well as Europe, calypso carries out the significance of its name, which means to conceal. The original bearer of this pretty name was Calypso, a goddess in Greek mythology, who was accustomed to keep her affairs hidden from the public eye.

Oddly, it is the clumsy bumble-bee that visits these small blossoms, but his short tongue is doubtless just as well adapted to the calypso flower as the incredibly long one of the great moth is to the eleven-inch tube of the snow-white orchid of Madagascar.

INDEX

2.2
2.1
3-3
4-3
4-7
5-3
7-6
7-7
8-4
13-1
13-6
14-4
14-6
16-1
17-6
19-3
20-3